'What Can I Do?'

'What Can I Do?'

Citizen Strategies
for
Nuclear Disarmament

ELIZABETH WOODWORTH

CREAM BOOKS   Victoria, Canada

Distributed by:
Gordon Soules Book Publishers Ltd.
1916 Pike Place - #620
Seattle, WA 98101 U.S.A.
Tel: (604) 922-6588
Fax: (604) 688-5442

Published by
CREAM BOOKS,
3909 Persimmon Dr.
Victoria, B.C.
Canada   V8P 3R8

Canadian Cataloguing in Publication Data
   Woodworth, Elizabeth M. (Elizabeth Margaret), 1943-
   What can I do?

   Bibliography: p.
   Includes index

   1. Nuclear disarmament. 2. Nonviolence. 3. Conflict
   management. 4. Peace. I. Title.
JX1974.7.W663   1987   327.1'74   C87-091202-X
ISBN 0-9692928-0-5

Cover design by David Litzenberger

Printed and bound in Canada by
MANNING PRESS LIMITED, Sidney, B.C.

To all who love the privilege of life;

and to

my mother,

the memory of my father,

and Claud, the soul of patience.

CONTENTS

Contents

Contents

PREFACE

This is a book about problem-solving. It is about what we in the West can do to repair a state of enmity with the Eastern bloc. Considerations of which side is right or wrong, which side free or unfree, will not be discussed. The object is to find a way of sharing the globe in a contracted and peaceful co-existence. If one side can prepare itself to approach the other with realistic and constructive and earnest proposals for peace, then it should empower itself to do so.

We in the West are individually capable of wanting to pursue such a course, and as individuals have the collective potential to require it of our leaders. The key is for large numbers of people to understand the obstacles in their own thinking which have been contributing to the aggregate problem we now face. The situation is not difficult to understand, but the confusion is widespread.

When any frightening problem, such as the proliferation of nuclear weapons, looms large in a culture's consciousness, there is a strong tendency to address the problem by attacking it, as one would shoot at a charging tiger. This habit of employing a greater violence to subdue a lesser one has played a decisive role in human history. But the nuclear weapons problem *is* human violence; it is the spirit and essence of human violence distilled into a technologically perfect form. To address this *particular* problem, therefore, requires a 180-degree about-face in our traditional approach to threat control. It requires a displacement of our attention from what we fear most to the challenge of discovering what we *do most want* for ourselves.

This involves understanding a rather delicate paradox. In thinking about nuclear holocaust, we project terribly frightening images into the mind's eye. If, on the one hand, we encourage these images — give them internal life — they grow, and as preoccupation with them develops, desperate action is more frequently contemplated. The possibility of war thus grows into the probability of war.

If, on the other hand, we do *not* entertain images of this very *real* threat, the energy which is desperately needed to deal with the problem will not come alive in us.

This paradox of the human imagination is at the heart of the nuclear issue, and to traverse the difficulty safely will require, above all, balance in our approach. It is like walking a tightrope, in which one may err towards one side or the other. The analogy may be carried further: any idea of falling which is allowed to enter the mind detracts from the concentration that is vital to the crossing.

The ingredients for success are thus balance and the determination to reach safety. True balance can only be achieved if, while being deeply concerned for the present danger of the planet, we are simultaneously capable of projecting and maintaining positive images for the future of mankind on earth. The direction things will now take, whether towards a golden age of global cooperation, or to a world in smoking embers, comes down to the quality of image-creation that each human being has the faith to project.

Each one of us, every day, touches everyone in his environment with the power and energy of his own orientation to life. And each one of us has the power of choice to tip the scales of his own creative imagination towards love, beauty, and progress, or towards fear, ugliness, and ruin. The images that prevail in consciousness are within our control, but only if we realize that we have the uniquely human power to stand back from our images and monitor them.

Each person who chooses hope over cynicism casts a vital vote in the destiny of the human spirit, and tips the planetary scales towards an assured future for mankind. We are all equally important in this respect, and the whole is the sum of the parts.

The heads of nuclear states are trapped with the lonely and frightening responsibility for preventing the ultimate disaster. Without a strong upward pressure, without a unified voice for decisive and constructive action from the mass of humanity below them, they remain stuck in the images of conflict and violence. Thus we *all* need to become involved in conquering these images, and we will live or die by the quality of our commitment.

Imagine a team of mountaineers, roped together and clinging to an icy precipice high on a mountain wall. Each critically important step must be placed precisely and securely, with a keen awareness of the price of error. Concentration is absolute: every movement is directed simply and elegantly towards survival as the team edges towards its goal of safety.

The purpose of this book is to produce in the reader the clear and magnified awareness of the mountaineer. It will pursue, step by step, the logic which we must together grasp if the world is to abandon its suicidal dependence on nuclearism. At the same time, it will identify and set to one side the irrelevant and confusing thoughts that have been cluttering our minds and clouding our visions of survival. When our vision has cleared our focus will change, and the emphasis on bombs will dissolve away.

The approach of this book will be to address only the parts of the nuclear issue that are *within our power to control*. All that we can do, ultimately, is to bring to our own attitudes a healthy and balanced perspective on world affairs. If we can achieve a genuine attitude of fairness and objectivity towards the Soviets, and a respect for their problems — if we can gain an overview of what *both* sides require — then we might induce a change in their attitudes as well. Such would be an act of true world leadership. We have nothing to lose by trying.

But if we are to even begin to try, we must first gain access to the political energy which is buried under a mass cultural repression of the awesome consequences of nuclear holocaust. This book guides the reader through these psychic blocks against nuclearism into an awareness of himself as the ultimate unit, or source, of political power. As a more considered understanding of political power develops, personal feelings of weakness and helplessness give way to a new sense of political strength, and to a corresponding willingness to deal with the problem from the individual level.

The problem in question centers around the fact that not only have arms control treaties historically failed to reduce or even limit nuclear weapons, but they have actually spurred arms development to mutually agreed new levels. Each increment makes survival on earth less certain.

In Part IV this book offers the reader the tools of democratic expression for survival in the nuclear age. It provides peoples of Western nuclear nations with the civilized means of regaining democratic control over the defense policies of their governments. The tools in question form an inventory of negotiation principles and nonviolent action techniques which may be used in persuading Western governments to get serious about *delivering* bilateral arms reductions with the Soviets. Forty years have shown that this will not happen until the people below get more serious about living than the people on top are preoccupied with supremacy.

ACKNOWLEDGEMENTS

I am absolutely certain that this book would never have reached publication had it not been for the encouragement and support I received during the manuscript phase. I am particularly indebted to Claud Heggie, Dr. David Bowering, Anne Carrow, my brother Garth Woodworth, Nancy de Candole and the late Dr. Corry de Candole, Susan and Keijo Isomaa, Alison Spriggs, Eevan Walker, Dr. Nick Schmitt, Jim and Hap Bramley, Dr. Tim Johnstone, David Litzenberger, with particular thanks to Dr. Elinor D. U. Powell, for the confidence that they demonstrated in both me and the manuscript.

Part I

Preparing to Look

CHAPTER 1

THE RUNAWAY ARMS RACE:
Inescapable Dilemma or Fragile System?

We all, as citizens of the planet, and regardless of our nationality, face a disconcerting predicament in which the forces at work are aligned roughly as follows:

1. U.S. and Soviet leaders, as spokesmen for rival powers of conflicting ideology, are locked in a struggle for world economic resources and a race for third world political support. A dynamic of enmity prevails, featuring mutual mistrust, mutually projected hostilities, and mutual fear of aggression.

2. Large-scale conventional warfare in support of this struggle has thus far been avoided by the unacceptable threat of escalation to nuclear war. Nuclear weapons themselves have no actual war-fighting use: their only plausible use is to deter the other side from using them first.

3. Technological advances, such as multiple warheads and automated communications and delivery systems, have produced such a complex network of nuclear products that strategists are finding it increasingly difficult to agree on deployment policies. Small weapons, such as the Cruise Missile, are destabilizing to the contracted and verifiable limitations on the arms race that were negotiated in the SALT I and SALT II treaties. In addition, there is strong rivalry between the U.S. Army, Navy, and Air Force for nuclear dollars.

4. The resulting headlong rush for nuclear "equality" has, by virtue of its massive acceleration of national debts, so destabilized the world economy that political tensions conducive to war

have been generated by these debts alone. But the overwhelming size and power of national defense industries produces an economic momentum that would be very difficult to reverse or to even slow down.

5. This daily growth in world arsenals increases the risk of nuclear war, not simply because there are more weapons, but because they are so much more in mind. And that about 40 countries are expected to be able to make the bomb by 1995 can only tip the scales further in the direction of our undoing.

6. Once a nuclear war begins, it is generally agreed — and particularly by Soviet strategists — that escalation to all-out war would be inevitable. Once having begun, calling it off would depend largely upon the intactness of Soviet-American communications links, and very few precautions have been taken to protect these.[1]

7. As tensions persist and deepen over the super-power race for global dominion, a captive world audience of concerned individuals waits anxiously by. Individual uneasiness takes the varying forms of helplessness, fatalism, indifference, and despair. This individual futility has undermined the confidence necessary for action, resulting in a largely paralyzed, unmobilized world public.

8. In short, the direction and energy of our orientation to the problem is extremely dangerous. We stand to lose everything — not just our own lives, but all our time-wrought institutions and inventions; all the humanity of our music, literature, and art; the innocent creatures of the animal kingdom; and perhaps above all, the green and sustaining earth itself.

*   *   *

The complex of forces described above combines to form the most difficult challenge that has ever beset mankind, and it is imperative that we rise to it, and quickly. Whether or not we will rise to it in time depends upon whether enough of us will come to see the problem as one which must be tackled from the individual level. And for the individual to interpret it as truly *his* problem, he must first learn to view the problem in manageable terms.

It is with this in mind that we are about to explore the new concept of the nuclear predicament as a *system*. So far it has been perceived as a kind of superstitious horror which one day might visit us like a punishing medieval plague.

When people speak of systems they are commonly referring to useful, functional entities which serve them in positive ways. Such systems are either essential to man, as is the digestive system, or they enhance his interests, as do the telephone and the refrigerator. A fundamental thing about a system, as anyone who is writing a cheque for automobile repairs will know, is that when one essential part breaks down, the whole system is impaired. Similarly with the body: each part must work in order to achieve the integrity of the whole, which is health.

It is interesting that we do not think in terms of systems when it comes to certain other kinds of organized phenomena, such as those which threaten our lives. For centuries, earthquakes, fires, floods, famines, and plagues were interpreted as catastrophic visitations, or as punishments inflicted by an angry god. However, once we began to analyze the components of these unwelcome events, they soon yielded to our understanding and control. For example, once the life cycle of the Anopheles mosquito was understood, malaria was seen to derive from part of a system — a system which could be readily impaired by filling in the swamps where mosquitoes breed.

A forest fire, too, can be seen as a natural system requiring a particular set of conditions: a source of ignition; a progressive supply of dry fuel; and the continuous availability of oxygen. This system may be disrupted by each of several means: by the prevention of ignition; by the introduction of water or firebreaks;

or by the use of explosives to create a temporary vacuum which interrupts the essential supply of oxygen.

Any set of conditions which is required to produce an undesirable effect may be seen as a kind of system operating in reverse, to achieve not a purpose, but a threat. But the set of interacting components is just as prone to disruption when a system is acting against our interests as when it is acting in favour of them.

So the key point about systems is that they are vulnerable to breakdown (if we like them) or disruption (if we do not). In our positively-functioning systems we discourage breakdown by maintenance and repair, while in our negatively-functioning systems, such as the insect destruction of crops, we introduce a disruptive factor such as a pesticide. Though some undesirable systems are particularly resistant to disruption, once the components have been identified and their interactions understood, a vulnerability usually becomes apparent, at which point the system becomes fragile, or breakable by man. A case in point is the new technology of earthquake control. The tidal wave is still at large, however — as is the volcano, and the threat of nuclear annihilation.

*   *   *

Let us now turn our attention to the nuclear arms race. This modern phenomenon conforms to a dictionary[2] definition as "system" as "a group of interacting, interrelated, or interdependent elements forming or regarded as forming a collective entity". Furthermore, this entity — the arms race — has energy, and produces results.

The big quetion is, is this system acting in favour of our interests, or against them? As we cannot know whether a future war awaits us or not, the best we can do to answer this question is to analyze the benefits and risks that seem to attend the system.

To be able to look at the nuclear military system impartially, however, we must first free our minds from the standard assumption that nuclear weapons are here to stay, and that we must learn to live with them. We should instead bear in mind that we created them, and that we may be capable of discarding them — of disrupting the system we have made from them — should we decide that it is not in our interests to maintain it. The assumption that the arms race is beyond human control is just that — a dangerous, pessimistic assumption — and like others of its kind, if it is taken to heart it is apt to be self-realizing.

Before proceeding to the benefits and risks of nuclearism, it might lend perspective to the topic to first identify the purpose of the system as its advocates see it. What is its alleged function?

It is here important to understand that the nuclear system was not methodically devised from conception to completion in the same manner as a building, for example, which is designed by an architect to serve a specific purpose. On the contrary, when the Pandora's Box of atomic fission was first blasted open in New Mexico in 1945, and the key soon obtained by the Soviet Union, the world was suddenly and unwittingly propelled into the nuclear arms race. But the arms race, as a competition, was never vested with any planned objectives, though objectives have since been contrived by strategists to defend its utility. At bottom it evolved as a natural history system of checks and balances in military power. To put it simply, the system grew in spite of us.

Nonetheless, nuclear advocates have devised a kind of after-the-fact justification for the system, which is that it serves to deter both conventional and nuclear military aggression between the USA and the USSR. In their view, its after-the-fact function is to preserve world peace. In this book this view will frequently be referred to as the "nuclear arms race military system" (or as "nuclearism" for short) of damping international disputes.

An abbreviated list of the observable benefits and risks is presented in the table below.

THE NUCLEAR ARMS SYSTEM
OF MAINTAINING WORLD PEACE

Benefits

1. No large-scale conventional world conflict has erupted since 1945. A great potential loss in military lives has been averted.

2. Nuclear weapons, because of their undesirable usability, have deterred actual use, thereby providing security against nuclear war.

3. NATO's first-use policy has prevented Warsaw Pact aggression in Europe.

4. The armaments industry stimulates the economy and provides considerable employment.

Risks

1. Surreptitious U.S.-Soviet economic and political conflict in world trouble-spots continually threatens the use of force leading to nuclear war. All life on the planet is at daily risk.

2. Usability, if not perfectly contained, will lead to actual use. The world is less secure now than it was before 1945.

3. If NATO deterrence fails and conflict develops, escalation will probably lead to all-out nuclear war.[3]

4a. Defense employment dollars would provide twice as many jobs in the civilian sector.[4]

4b. Armaments spending has created a huge U.S. federal deficit and has diverted money away from human services. Resulting inflation has deformed both the U.S. and the world economy.

5. Horizontal proliferation of nuclear arms to other countries has created the risks of non-superpower and terrorist use.

6. Modernization and miniaturization of the weapons, by decreasing the time available for decision-making, increases the incentive towards "first-strike" and "launch on warning". This undermines deterrence, the principle function that the weapons are held to serve.

7. The ever-present threat of holocaust reduces our confidence in the future, and undermines the quality of life.

8. The destructive potential of the weapons is so frightening that it impairs our ability to think logically about them.

TABLE 1

The risks enumerated in the table above obviously outweigh the benefits in number — but more important, the worst risk (annihilation) is of a completely different order of magnitude than the best benefit (avoidance of conventional war). To claim the avoidance of *nuclear* war as a benefit of nuclear weapons is absurd and self-negating, especially when viewed within the possibility of our having a choice as to whether to deploy them *at all*.

This book will proceed from the judgement that the risks imposed upon the planet by nuclear arms are unacceptable and unjustifiable. This is ultimately a subjective judgement, and people will differ. Those who differ regard the arms race as a positive thing, believing that we can exercise enough caution and control to make deterrence work until we either achieve a global unity, or find a new approach to conflict resolution. But it is regarded negatively by those whose imagination is alive to the destructive potential of the weapons, and who are mindful of Murphy's ever-present law that "if something can go wrong, something will go wrong."

Recent U.S. opinion polls have shown that with developing arms technology and increasing expenditures, greater numbers of people are holding the second view. And there is indeed the larger question of world opinion beyond the six nuclear nations of today: the United States, the USSR, Great Britain, France, China, India, and also probably Israel and Pakistan. Certainly the world's remaining 160-odd countries have everything to lose and nothing to gain by this contagion of nuclear warheads. What we have, then, is a system of preserving peace that most people perceive as acting against their interests. And as there can be no objective measure of the success that the nuclear arms race will bring to the future, we conclude that the only available measure is the present subjectivity of a frightened world public.

*   *   *

We have presented the case that as a system the nuclear arms race is functioning against the interests of mankind. Like any other organized and threatening problem, it breaks down into individual components, any one of which, or combination of which, might yield to disruptive strategies.

Obviously such strategies are not likely to emerge from those who support the arms race, or whose livelihood is dependent upon it.[5] The energy can only come from those who have a simple, uncomplicated wish to remove the threat: in short, from the great collective of concerned individuals.

Even supposing a unified public will were to emerge in the West, how could it disrupt the nuclear military system other than by unilateral disarmament?

It should be understood here very clearly that this book does *not* advocate unilateral disarmament. Instead it advocates that we urge American leadership to take a balanced and objective overview of the American-Soviet pattern of pessimism and fear, and make a resolute attempt to overcome the existing psychological stalemate. Consider the following:

> "Then there is the so-called 'image of the enemy.' This is universal. All social animals, including humans, feel distrust of a stranger; and when two groups get into a rivalry situation, distrust escalates very rapidly until the rival group conforms to this image of the enemy . . Thus, the image of the enemy blocks efforts to resolve the conflict, because like all images it acts like the filtering lens that lets through what confirms it, and de-emphasizes what fails to fit it. The enemy is seen as untrustworthy. As President Reagan said, 'the Russians ae liars and cheats.' I am afraid, in the diplomatic world, everyone is a liar and a cheat. You may remember the characterization of an ambassador: an honest man sent abroad to lie for his country. But who wants to sit down and talk with a liar and a cheat, so the first thing you do is break off communications, as we are doing with the Russians. They've got to be good, they've got to stop the trouble in Poland, they've got to get out of Afghanistan, before we'll talk to them. This ridiculous posture rests on the assumption that reducing nuclear arms is a favor that we are offering to the Russians, instead of realizing that it would be a favor to both sides."[6]

That the stalemate must be overcome is abundantly clear, but stalemates do not just go away: they must be negotiated away. The United States, as an open society with a centuries-old background of liberalism, would seem to have certain advantages over the USSR — a closed society (though now emerging), a relative newcomer to world power, and a country governed on recent and hitherto untested organizational principles. So Western leadership, in dealing with Soviet guardedness and secrecy, should do so from the same spirit of fairness, optimism, and dialogue that gradually fostered its own institutions. The United States must not lose sight of its own original meaning by mindlessly pursuing this spiralling game of mistrust and hostility — the kind of game which when played between individuals is seen as near-sighted and immature. A skilled, enlightened, and determined U.S. diplomacy would be needed to overcome the impasse that prevails in U.S.-Soviet relations.

One of the reasons for this impasse is that the arms race has become so strategically complicated that it is now almost impossible to negotiate an effective and verifiable arms limitation treaty.[7] In spite of this difficulty, however, there are several ways that the United States could take the initiative to restore confidence to negotiations, and to minimize dangerous misunderstandings while treaty developments are underway:

1. American leadership could take a first, goodwill step in the withdrawal of a weapon of particular concern to the Soviets (such as the Pershing II), and back this move with the declared intention of removing a second weapon if the USSR will reciprocate in the meantime by withdrawing a weapon of agreed equal value.

2. American leadership could propose a simple, quickly-negotiable interim agreement; for example, that for every new warhead deployed on either side, another warhead of similar value would be subtracted from that side. This would achieve an effective freeze, and would permit technology to progress while efforts were being made to draft a more comprehensive treaty.[8]

3. American leadership could propose to the USSR the idea of a joint crisis management center to sidestep the present vulnerability of the "hot-line". A jointly manned crisis management center would permit the shared examination and discussion of tensions during a developing crisis.[9]

It is obvious that these measures can only be taken by leadership. However, this cannot be left to chance: there really is not time to wait around for elections and policy changes to possibly occur. Instead, it is a matter of applying a sustained and mobilized public pressure on *whatever* leadership is in power. (How to apply a clean and effective pressure will be dealt with extensively in the last section of this book.)

This brings us to the most vital yet vulnerable link in the arms race system: the system depends utterly upon a passive, acquiescent, tax-paying public in both super-powers. No substantial force has ever been brought to bear on either leadership to negotiate a certain and verifiable end to the arms race. And not a single arms limitation treaty has been ratified since 1972.

Our one hope for the disruption of the arms race is that the American public will come to its collective senses, recognize itself as an *indispensable* link in the nuclear military system, and mobilize itself to pressure its leadership to court the Soviets for peace. What has anyone got to lose? If the effort fails, and Soviet cynicism proves to be altogether impenetrable, at least our certain knowledge of that fact will be no more dangerous than is our current untested suspicion of it.

We have identified the one essential player in the arms race system who has both a) a vested interest in disrupting the system; and b) the power to disrupt it. That player is the cornerstone of all national policies — the obedient, unquestioning citizen. We shall now turn our attention to the obstacles which have thus far prevented this key performer from releasing its collective energy against the threat of its own extinction.

CHAPTER 2

THE STRUCTURE OF APATHY:
A Break in the Vicious Circle

A recent public opinion poll showed that some 50% of Americans believe that they will die within five years in a nuclear war.

Usually, if anything will bind a group of people together in a unified purpose, it will be a common threat. That modern man has not risen unanimously against this greatest threat of all time may be seen, therefore, as a rather remarkable phenomenon. What is impairing a unified response to this urgent matter of survival?

On the face of it the disunity seems to stem from disagreement as to what actually constitutes the threat. Some have been conditioned by history to believe in "the enemy" — an outside rival group such as the Soviet Union — as constituting the root threat to our peace and security. Others believe that the bomb itself is the foremost threat to survival; still others, the military establishment; and so on.

Such disagreements, which have obscured an American vision of a clear and purposeful course of action, are nonetheless open to settlement. Settlements of this kind, though rare, are possible, and are most often reached during national emergencies when brilliance in leadership combines with public compliance to effect the necessary unity.

Statesmanship is the ability to lead the individual mind beyond its immediate concerns to an appreciation of the overview, or the "big picture". Thus the confusion of many small and differing points of view is replaced by the clarity of a detached assessment of the common good.

Statesmanship is also the ability to identify far-sighted objectives that will serve the common good, and to apply them, through educational leadership, to politically fragmented populations. This requires unusual care, vision, and energy.

Why has there been so little evidence of Western statesmanship in recent decades? The answer is that in a democracy, individual perceptions percolate through to the top. As George Bernard Shaw once observed, "democracy ensures that the people will get no better government than they deserve." So ultimately, individual consciousness contains both the source and the solution to American participation in the arms race. And statesmen, after all, are individuals themselves, and it is to individual citizens that they must successfully appeal.

*   *   *

Most people know that the world could be destroyed by nuclear war within thirty minutes. But month after month, the U.S. Government courts disaster by engaging in provocative conflicts with the Soviet Union. And the people watch the evening news, holding their breath at each new crisis, as though helpless.

When any other creature is confronted with a life and death situation, the perception of danger is linked at lightning speed to a survival response. What is aborting our survival response to this hovering, sinister threat? This is a question of absolutely crucial importance, as our survival depends upon the rekindled awareness of an immediate and lethal danger.

Our failure to respond does not lie in a single problem, as for example, a furnace which will not run because of an empty oil tank. Our paralysis is rather a collection of problems which have evolved over time, each one contributing its share to the breakdown. It is like an old heating system in an abandoned house, which has several separate and distinct problems that must be identified and solved individually before the furnace will work: an electrical short in the power supply; a blockage in the fuel line; and a broken fanbelt. The mechanic, in approaching the furnace, knows that he must solve first things first — that he must begin by getting power to the furnace in order for it to have a chance of running at all. Once the motor is running, he finds that the fuel supply line has been dented, and finally that hot air is not being circulated by the fan.

The purpose of the furnace example is to show that multiple problems must be approached in the right order if solutions are to become possible. And though it requires logical thinking to establish that order, the situation does break down into single problems that are, in themselves, simple and easily repaired.

So it is with the malfunctioning human response to the nuclear threat. The first problem — the one that logically precedes all others on the way to the solution — is that we are disconnected from our feelings about the bomb. The first thing that must be established, therefore, is emotional reconnection (just like the power to the furnace), because feeling is the source of all energy and vitality. And feeling, energy, and determination are needed in abundance to solve the very real but separate political and economic problems that drive the arms race.

Several factors have been identified as contributing to the cultural breakdown of the psychic forces of survival:

1. *Disconnection*: The "power supply" in the human being is the will to live — the life force — and when it is healthy and strong it is experienced with keen emotion in its basic manifestations: in the urgency of sexual union; in the wonder of birth; and in the intense struggle to resist death.

It was emotion, in all its forms — rage, love, fear, sadness, joy revulsion, delight — that guided us through the eons of evolution. Emotions are the feelings in consciousness that attract us to safety and continued existence, and repel us from danger and extinction. They are our biological pathfinders — our survival command signals.

But here we are in the 1980's, emotionally connected to our immediate lives, yet anesthetized to the volcanic weapons that loom in our midst. While we go about our business, rapid and uncontrolled expansion of these weapons steadily progresses. With each new weapon the planet becomes more of a powder-keg, but we do not hold this menace in consciousness. That we do not allow this awareness of danger, this acuity of the mountaineer on the precipice, is the numbness,[1] which like hypothermia to the mountaineer, robs us of our will to survive and our drive to reach safety.

How is it that in relation to nuclear death we are so blasé, so casual, so readily fatalistic? Certainly a large part of it is that because we assume the problem is beyond our control, we regard worrying about it as futile — a reasonable conclusion if the assumption is right. Fortunately, though, many good minds have refused to buy this assumption, and have been at work devising ingenious individual strategies to beat the problem; these strategies will be detailed in later chapters.

But there are deeper, unconscious influences at work, and to overcome them they must first be seen, or made conscious. These have been identified in the literature of psychology, and it is interesting to observe them at work in oneself.

The first is that not only are we repressing what we have heard so many times about the bomb, but that we have never been able to accurately imagine it all.

2. *Failure to Imagine the Real:* Psychologists believe that human beings are protected from an overload of emotional suffering by certain classical defense mechanisms, including repression, denial, projection, and isolation. These unconscious mechanisms selectively screen out enough potential misery to allow the conscious mind the comfort and enjoyment it needs to sustain, on balance, the will to live.

The particular stresses of modern life have produced some new defense mechanisms, some new subconscious tricks to limit our awareness of all that is real. One is that with antibiotics and public sanitation, though death still comes to everyone, it is not the immediate domestic presence that it once commonly was. Many people have never seen a human corpse. We have so little experience of the actuality of death that it is more an abstraction than a reality. We talk of death, we watch it on television, but the direct experience of it is usually limited to a hospitalized elder. It is the exception to confront death in a young person, which is regarded as tragic and premature. So ordinary death, or what Kurt Vonnegut refers to as "plain old death", is now very well controlled in developed countries. And though it will claim each of us at some unknown time, death seems, during most of life, strangely hypothetical.

When a personal sense of death is hypothetical, how threatening can a nuclear warhead be? We do not have the raw material of experience from which to build its image. So the hideous impact of a nuclear explosion on a city like San Francisco (or Leningrad) cannot easily be visualized, because there is no bank of death experience, in either immediate circumstances, or from the bomb itself, upon which to draw. It is precisely this remoteness of everyday death — our very control over it — which could, ironically, lead to a mass human destruction, a destruction we must be able to vividly imagine in order to prevent.

So the inability to "imagine the real" (Martin Buber's phrase) is central to an understanding of the emotional weakness with which we meet nuclear weapons. To revitalize our emotional integrity — our wholeness and toughness and hardiness — it will be necessary in a later chapter to invite our natural feelings of indignation, anger, and fear. These are strongly motivating feelings, and it is their energy which might yet save us, but in order for them to awaken with authority and determination the mind must first decide to make itself completely receptive to the aftermath of an atomic blast. This willingness to know and feel will make us whole and alive again, like the creatures of the forest, which are captives of alertness.

2. *Habituation:* Another psychological explanation for emotional numbing has been advanced by Dr. Jerome D. Frank:

> "When the enormous destructive power of nuclear weapons threatens to break into awareness, its impact is weakened by at least two psychological mechanisms. One is the mechanism of denial, which is often talked about. There is another that we do not hear so much about, a very important mechanism, habituation. Like all living creatures, we humans stop attending to stimuli when they persist unchanged over a period of time. Survival in the wild required not only the ability to detect any changes in the environment, but also to ignore them if they persisted without creating any actual danger. If an animal kept attending to every environmental stimulus, its capacity to sense new dangers would be swamped. Therefore it just stops attending to them. We do the same thing. The first atomic bomb dropped on Hiroshima created a worldwide shock wave that stimulated intense efforts to ban nuclear weapons. As decades passed without further nuclear explosions, the nuclear threat slipped from attention, with only occasional flurries of concern. We have to thank our current president for creating one such flurry now by suddenly making the weapons salient again, but most of the time they simply sink into the background. They are part of the ground rather than the figure, as psychologists say, and that makes it very difficult to keep them in mind." [2]

Not being able to keep the danger in mind is the greatest danger of all. This is perhaps the most important point in this book. For the individual to truly and meaningfully understand the nuclear problem, he must start with a new perception of where the danger actually begins. The enemy is not the weapons themselves — they do not build themselves or shoot themselves off. The danger is our own, personal, individual apathy, multiplied by hundreds of millions of apathies, which together not only fail to discourage — but actually *finance* — a relatively small group of "bomb managers" (sometimes referred to as the "nuclear priesthood") in the pursuit of their dark game.

It is like the mountaineer again. The climber's greatest challenge is not the mountain but himself. Danger is a background condition of life, be it a cliff-face, a slippery sidewalk, or a weapons arsenal. These kinds of things are always out there, and not necessarily subject to our control. What *is* within our control, however, is the quality of our response: the will, determination, judgement and imagination with which we meet these hazards.

Diagram 1 below represents the structure of the view, commonly held, that the greatest problem is an "out there" problem — the nuclear arsenal itself. Whenever this assumption is held, the behind-the-scenes logic of the subconscious senses that the danger is remote and beyond the control of the individual. If the problem emerges into consciousness, "What can I do?" is the

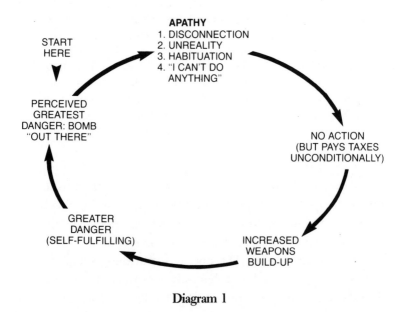

APATHY
1. DISCONNECTION
2. UNREALITY
3. HABITUATION
4. "I CAN'T DO ANYTHING"

START HERE

PERCEIVED GREATEST DANGER: BOMB "OUT THERE"

NO ACTION (BUT PAYS TAXES UNCONDITIONALLY)

GREATER DANGER (SELF-FULFILLING)

INCREASED WEAPONS BUILD-UP

Diagram 1

standard reply, and the problem is pushed underground again. The resulting political inactivity of these millions of affected people permits a bilateral arms build-up that is spurred by a seemingly unlimited technology. With no political brake (millions of outraged people) on its momentum, this build-up advances by leaps and bounds, and thereby the danger grows. The circle is vicious and closed.

Diagram 2 represents a shift in emphasis. Here the greatest danger is perceived as an "in here" danger, that each person "owns" as a problem within his control. The danger is apathy — the combination of disconnection, unreality, habituation, and "I can't *do* anything." When this shift takes place, the individual suddenly sees himself as central to the problem, and connected to everyone else by it. Each life is worth saving, and each person must save his own.

Seeing onself as central to the problem creates a flip side of the coin which puts one in control of the solution. Just one person's control, granted, but each "one person" who takes control weights the outcome to this ultimate problem in a positive direction. *This insight into one's individual relevance constitutes the beginning of true personal responsibility.*

In becoming responsible one picks up a double-edged sword: one is not only the source of conditions as they are, but by the same token is dramatically empowered to change them. The *burden* of responsibility, when thus turned around, changes into the delightful prospect of — far from being helpless — being *able* to respond.

If this insight into one's own contribution to apathy is held up squarely and steadily to scrutiny, it should lead, by inevitable logic, to a decision to respond. Being responsible and the act of responding (as in respond to a stimulus) are thus seen to be one and the same thing, as the words would suggest.

When apathy is recognized as the enemy, the direction for a solution is suddenly straightforward. The goal is revitalization, and this energy must come, as in the animal kingdom, from a direct perception of the danger. To directly perceive the danger one must look at it, steadily and with courage, until the horror of it dawns, adrenalin flows, and strong intention is born. This total physical adrenalin response *must* occur — at least initially — and when it does, far from being viewed as neurotic anxiety or as a valium deficiency, it should be welcomed as the first healthy step towards a collective recovery. Then begins the excitement of *wanting* to act — of wanting to meet others who *care*, who are alive and involved and determined to help. As increasing numbers of people achieve this reintegration of their own will to survive, more and more action is taken against these deadly weapons, and less likelihood of nuclear holocaust results. The vicious circle is broken:

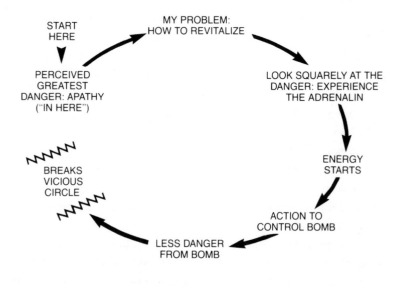

Diagram 2

This willingness to look directly at the horror of the bomb might be described as the awakening of nuclear courage. "Courage" is a fine word, coming from the Middle English "corage", meaning "the heart as the seat of feeling". In French, "le coeur" means both "heart" and "courage". When an action takes courage, a person has to tolerate the pounding of his heart, but it doesn't hurt — it keeps on beating. And that's what it's all about.

CHAPTER 3

HOW THE BOMB WORKS:
A Simple Look at Ultimate Energy

Though for centuries mankind has been awed by the force and violence of nature, nothing he has ever seen even remotely approaches the viciously incinerating blast of a large thermonuclear bomb. In splitting the atom and building the bomb, man has transformed the very soul of matter into a savage, poisonous energy which is foreign to earth and its life processes. Its lethal radioactivity persists for hundreds of thousands of years. Our natural history has equipped us with neither the genetic memory to sense the fury of the blast, nor the physical immunity to ward off its poisons.

It is of particular importance, therefore, that the peoples of earth should grasp and bear in mind the uncanny magnitude of nuclear fission and fusion reactions. And though it took physicists several decades to pry the atom apart — and its resistance to being thus toyed with collapsed with a vengeance — the process is not in principle difficult to understand. The difficulty lay, rather, in the technology required to deal with the *size* of the atom; the *nature* of what was undertaken, and why it has such immense significance for the future of life on this planet is a matter of relative simplicity.

This chapter will explain in elementary terms what makes a nuclear reaction so special, so uniquely powerful. *That* a nuclear blast produces millions of times more energy than does a conventional chemical one (given materials of similar volume) is difficult to really credit until one sees *why* it does so. Understanding the "why" will remove any further temptation to think of a nuclear detonation as merely a "bomb", which is an old word for a large firecracker, whereas a nuclear blast is more like an exploding sun. And there are now more than 50,000 of them available for our "security".

Briefly, then, the world, and all its life, is made up from about ninety different basic natural elements. Elements (such as carbon, gold, and oxygen) are the simplest of substances because all the atoms within each element are identical. An atom, similarly, is the smallest unit of an element which still retains the characteristics of that element. So there are atoms of carbon, gold, oxygen, and so on.

Atoms are identical, or of the same element, when they have equal numbers of protons in their core, or nucleus. In other words, they have the same "atomic number". A proton is a positively charged particle of subatomic size which is always present, though in varying numbers, in the nucleus of an atom.

Also present in the nucleus is the neutron, another subatomic particle, but carrying no (or neutral) electrical charge. The combined number of protons and neutrons (which are roughly equal in most atoms) determines the mass (or weight) of an element,

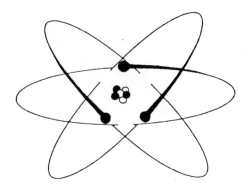

Diagram 3.
An atom of the element lithium.

and is expressed as the "mass number". Predictably, a light element such as oxygen has a low mass number, 16, whereas lead has 207.2.

The third and final particle in this simplified picture is the electron, a negatively-charged particle *of much smaller mass* than either the proton or neutron. The electrons orbit around the nucleus, and they equal the number of protons within it, so that each negative charge outside is balanced by a positive charge inside. The atom is assembled like a tiny model of the solar system, with as much relative space between the electrons and the nucleus as there is between the planets and the sun (Diagram 3).

The next order of matter above the atom is the molecule. A molecule is composed of two or more atoms, linked together by a common electron, and forming the smallest unit of a more complex substance called a compound. The molecule is the smallest unit of a compound (such as water, table salt, and hydrochloric acid) which retains the physical properties of that compound.

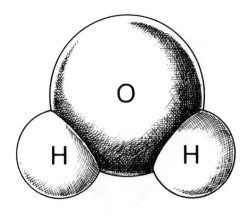

Diagram 4.

A molecule of the compound, water.

The force which holds an atom together in its configuration of electrons and protons, and similarly a number of atoms together in a molecule, is known as the *electromagnetic force*. Its action is based upon the fact that particles of the same electrical sign — be it positive or negative — utterly repel each other, whereas particles of opposing electrical signs irresistably attract one another. Anyone who has tried to touch together the positive ends of two bar magnets has felt this invisible force.

The electromagnetic force (EMF) is the glue of the universe at both the atomic and molecular levels in the structure of matter. It is this force which drives all chemical reactions. A chemical reaction is one in which a new substance (or substances) is produced because of a change in the way the atoms are bound together. This change in linkage involves an exchange of electrons only, and therefore occurs *outside* the nuclei of the atoms involved. For example, a new molecule of water is formed (H_2O) when two atoms of hydrogen and one atom of oxygen are combined through the sharing of two common electrons. This is a combination reaction; a decomposition (or breakdown) reaction occurs when a compound, such as mercuric oxide, is heated to produce the simpler substances mercury and oxygen — both elements. Some chemical reactions occur very slowly, such as the combining of iron and oxygen to form rust. Others occur quickly and violently, such as the explosion of dynamite. Fast or slow, they are all caused by the same electromagnetic force that we feel between the magnets.

Physicists used to believe that the electromagnetic force, operating outside the atom's nucleus, was the ultimate source of energy in nature. And so it was, *in nature*. At least on earth. The old conservation law of energy (energy can be neither created nor destroyed, but only transformed) held that though energy may be transformed by a chemical reaction, it would still be the same amount of energy. Similarly, the law of conservation of matter (matter can be neither created nor destroyed) held that though matter may be chemically changed from one substance to another, it would still amount to the same mass or weight.

Energy was energy, and mass was mass, and that was that.

In 1905, Albert Einstein came along and changed the world forever, because he interpreted matter and energy as being different forms of *the same thing*. He proved theoretically that mass (the nucleus of an atom, essentially) could be converted into energy, and that if its energy could be tapped, the result would equal the mass times the speed of light (186,000 miles per second) squared. In other words, $E = mc^2$.

The force which was defined by this classic formula is today referred to by physicists simply as "the strong force". To get an idea of its magnitude, consider that the nucleus of a heavy atom, such as uranium-235, is tightly packed with 92 protons and 143 neutrons. Now these protons, under any other circumstances, would not come anywhere near one another because of their mutual repulsion under the electromagnetic force. In spite of this, they remain closely bound together by an obviously far greater force.

If a single proton is fired at high speed toward the nucleus of a uranium atom, the proton will veer away from its target in a curving line, because it is so actively repelled by the 92 protons within the nucleus. However, when we do manage to fire a proton right up to the nucleus' doorstep — to within one ten-trillionth of a centimeter, which is the approximate breadth of the proton itself — suddenly a force which is 100 times as strong as the electromagnetic force seizes the approaching proton and clasps it right into the nucleus with the others. This force operates only at extremely close range, but once operative, it easily overcomes the electromagnetic force. It is now regarded as the ultimate force in nature, and is the phenomenon which is released during nuclear fission. Its yield, furthermore, correctly corresponds to the theoretical prediction of Einstein's formula, $E = mc^2$.

The strong force was first released by man during the 1930's, a period of very active experimentation with subatomic particles. It was discovered that when a neutron was forced into the nucleus of a uranium-235 atom, the balance between the strong force (which holds the nucleus together) and the electromagnetic force (which would like to break it apart) was disrupted by the sudden arrival of this new particle. The result was threefold: the nucleus shattered into several lighter atoms; there was a dramatic release of energy; and several free neutrons were left over. This splitting of the nucleus was called *fission*, which literally means "splitting into parts".

The release of these neutrons during fission gave rise to the idea that a chain reaction might be produced by the blast of liberated neutrons. Like the original proton, it was thought, these little bullet neutrons might go on to split more atoms, which in turn might release a new generation of free neutrons, and so on. This thinking was taking place in 1938-39, and it soon became apparent that a weapon of fantastic power was in the making, one that might well determine the outcome of World War II.

In practice, however, the chain reaction proved very difficult to produce. For one thing, there were only two materials which would fission reliably — uranium-235 and plutonium-239, and these were both hard to obtain. Uranium-235 accompanied the abundant uranium-238 in nature, but only in trace amounts, and their separation was expensive. Plutonium-239 had to be artificially manufactured from uranium-235 in a reactor, another highly complex process.

The next problem was that these laboriously assembled materials would not fission in a self-sustaining chain reaction unless they existed in suitably large chunks. In a small piece of uranium there is so much surface area relative to the size of the mass that many of the neutrons required to produce the chain reaction would escape uselessly into the air, fizzling out the chain reaction before it could develop into an explosion.

A piece of uranium large enough to permit the build-up of generations of fissioning nuclei within its bulk is said to have "critical mass". In making a controllable weapon, therefore, it was necessary to have a piece of uranium-235 (or plutonium-239) of *nearly* critical (or subcritical) mass, such that at a moment's notice it could be changed into a supercritical (or more than critical) mass, which would then instantly explode.

Two methods were devised to effect this control. The first was a kind of gun-barrel device, in which two separate subcritical masses were suddenly fired together by a small chemical charge to produce a mass of supercritical size. The second method was based on the fact that a slightly subcritical piece of uranium can be made supercritical by compressing it, which increases the ratio of the mass to the surface area. Accordingly, a subcritical quantity of uranium-235 (or plutonium-239) was placed in an enclosed sphere, surrounded by an outside layer of chemical explosives. To set it off, the chemical jacket was detonated, which produced a shock wave to compress the uranium, which then became supercritical. By adding an extra supply of neutrons at the same time, a fantastic explosion was generated.

By the time these wrinkles had been ironed out, Germany had been all but defeated, and the target for the experimental use of the weapon had shifted to Japan. On July 16, 1945, the first atomic explosion in history — the test weapon "Trinity" — was detonated at Alamogordo, New Mexico. The expected energy yield, which had been estimated in the range of 1000-5000 tons of TNT, was far exceeded by the astonishing 20,000-ton equivalent. A few weeks later two similar bombs were dropped on Hiroshima and Nagasaki to expedite the surrender of Japan.

The unexpected power of these few pounds of fissionable material has since been explained by the *time scale* of a fission reaction. Each generation of fissioning neutrons takes only one-hundredth of one-millionth of a second to reach and split another nucleus, which then releases at least two more neutrons, etc. Each time a nucleus splits, a small burst of violent energy is released into the mass, and these fissions multiply through the mass at the enormous rate of $2 \times 2 \times 4 \times 8 \times 16 \times 32 \times 64$, and so on.

How the Bomb Works

Fifty generations will have been completed within one-half of one-millionth of a second, each generation being at least twice the size of the one before. It is estimated that during a 58-generation fission reaction, 99.9% of the total energy is produced during the last seven generations.[1] When this seething mass "finally" explodes, it immediately becomes subcritical and stops fissioning. But in a total time of fifty-eight hundredths of a millionth of a second, as much energy has been released as would have been produced by the explosion of 100,000 tons of TNT.

In addition to this blast energy, the newly-formed lighter atoms, or "fission fragments", emit an energy of their own, which we are well familiar with as radioactivity. This high frequency electromagnetic energy takes the form of X rays, gamma rays, and beta particles, and it continues to radiate from the nuclei of these new atoms until a stable (or non-radioactive) nucleus has been re-established. Most of this radiation is released immediately, and though the rate of release declines steadily during the following days, total stability is not achieved in all of the 80 different kinds of fission fragments until millions of years have passed. This radioactive energy is referred to by physicists as "the weak force", and its effects upon life processes will be discussed later.

Fusion reactions are opposite to fission reactions in that the nuclei of very *light* atoms (e.g., hydrogen, which has one proton in the nucleus; duterium, with one proton and one neutron; and tritium, with one proton and two neutrons) are combined (or fused) into one heavier atom as a result of exposure to extremely high temperatures. Weight for weight, the materials used in fusion produce about three times as much energy as do those used in fission, and it is noteworthy that the relatively "clean" energy from the sun and the stars is actually an ongoing fusion reaction.

Fusion is difficult to achieve because it involves the bringing together of proton-inhabited nuclei, and therefore has the electromagnetic force working strongly against it. (Remember that in fission only a neutron penetrated the nucleus, so that it was not repelled by the disadvantage of a positive charge.) The only known energy that will force these hydrogen nuclei to merge has been temperatures in the tens of millions of degrees Centigrade range. Such temperatures excite the hydrogen atoms into a state of such intense, "popping" activity that they are driven into collisions with such enormous velocity that the proton repulsion is overcome and their nuclei fuse together. The result is the production of helium (with two protons in its nucleus) and a massive release of energy in the form of highly-accelerated free neutrons.

The only temperature on earth which will excite hydrogen to this degree is that produced by a fission explosion. A thermonuclear bomb, therefore, is one which utilizes both heat and fission to generate energy. It has at its core the same sphere of subcritical uranium-235, surrounded by the same jacket of chemical explosives. But encasing this is a further layer of a light fusionable mixture, such as lithium, tritium, or deuterium. And finally there is an outer envelope containing more fissionable fuel, such as uranium-238.

When the button is pushed, the chemical jacket is detonated to compress the uranium-235 at the core; this spontaneously fissions to produce the required heat; the heat triggers an intense fusion reaction in the surrounding light fuel mixture; and a huge blast of high-speed neutrons is discharged into the outer layer of uranium-238. These bullet-like neutrons have now attained sufficient speed to fission the abundant, naturally-occurring but previously unfissionable isotope, uranium-238. So the potential size of the explosion is now virtually infinite, with a destructive force limited only by the earth's ability to absorb the blast.

Though historically the electromagnetic force seemed to be the ultimate force of nature, we now recognize it as relative rather than absolute. We see this in the readiness of chemical bonds to form and reform in nature, and by how easily they yield to influences such as fire. And even a large conventional explosion,

such as a ton of TNT, produces only 5000 degrees Centigrade —
a yield which is proportionate to the strength of the EMF itself.

But the *strong* force, on the other hand, is the ultimate force of
the universe. It dwells quietly at the heart of all matter — the
glue of the universe, holding matter together and ensuring its
stability. It is the superforce upon which the permanence of the
atom and therefore the continuity of all creation is based. But
when this sleeping force of nature is prodded into wakefulness,
its power is as vicious and ugly as nature is beautiful. Its uncanny
destruction is measured in temperatures of unfathomable magnitude — tens of millions of degrees Centigrade — which otherwise occur only in the rare and brief phenomenon of the exploding supernova.

Both Einstein and Oppenheimer were adamantly opposed to
the development of the fission-fusion (or hydrogen) bomb. They
foresaw its unlimited destructive energy, which was measured
not in thousands of tons of TNT (or kilotons), like the fission
bomb, but in *millions* of tons of TNT (or megatons).

On November 1, 1952, the United States of America set off the
first hydrogen bomb, obliterating without trace a small island in
the South Pacific.

Man had taken over the destiny of the planet. He now held the
reins of power, the verdict of life or death over every living thing.
Are we, forty years later, to treat this as a matter of passing interest, as a "background" issue? Or are we to turn and face this mon-
strous aberration of our own making, this ghastly intruder into
the affairs of our beloved Earth?

Part II

Looking

CHAPTER 4

A VISIT TO ARMAGEDDON:
One Megaton Versus One City

Nobody really knows, once a nuclear war has begun, how extensive the bombing might be. But there would be several rather bleak conclusions to be drawn from the fact that war had begun at all. First, because nuclear war is "unthinkable", it would imply — barring a terrible accident — that the leaders had been operating under such extremely stressful conditions that rational judgement had failed them entirely. It is precisely such conditions, however, that have accompanied recent developments in the timing, accuracy, and location of nuclear warheads. The time now available to make decisions of ultimate importance during a crisis is in the order of minutes — six or seven. And by the time that even one weapon has been launched, things have already gone terribly wrong, because the whole purpose of the system of checks and balances between poised warheads is to *prevent* war. The principle of deterrence rests upon the *credibility of the usability* of the weapons, but if in fact they are ever used, deterrence will have utterly failed.

If acutely frayed nerves were to seek relief in action, it would not make much more sense to fire only one weapon than to fire all, because firing even one would immediately suggest to the enemy that all might be on the way. And even if a slow motion, blow-for-blow war were to begin, a decapitation strike aimed at Washington or Moscow would destroy the hot line and make it impossible for leaders to call off the war. Even if the leaders survived to discuss a truce over an intact hot line, they would be unable to reach many of their own military personnel. One high-altitude nuclear burst over the central United States is capable, via the electromagnetic pulse phenomenon, of shorting out electrical equipment over thousands of square miles. The whole internal chain of command could be plunged into a communications chaos. People at all levels would be in the dark: do we fire, or do we hold back and face imminent annihilation ourselves?

It comes down to a very simple situation. If two terrified enemies are facing each other across a dark forest clearing, each holding a hand grenade, what is the strongest temptation each feels at that moment? Upon this kind of reflection it is not difficult to see why most analysts conclude that there is little chance of a nuclear war remaining limited.

It is now time to look at the dark side of deterrence, at the genie escaping the bottle of man's control and turning against him — and then inflicting a scale of ruin monstrously disproportionate to the importance of any human conflict, now or ever.

To begin with, then, there are now more than 50,000 nuclear warheads in existence. These are held mainly by the two superpowers, but are also distributed among the NATO countries (American allies), the Warsaw Pact countries (Soviet allies), and Britain, France, China, India and probably Israel and Pakistan.

Within the United States alone, the many thousands of targets include: land-based ICBM's (intercontinental ballistic missiles), military bases, airports, fuel supply depots, hydroelectric stations, transportation terminals, arms factories, and seats of government. But even after every conceivable military target has been hit, there are still enough one-metaton (1-Mt.) bombs left over in the Soviet Union, that for all of them to be aimed at something (which is presumably why they are made), they would also have to be pointed at every U.S. population center down to 1500 people.

The bombs which were dropped on Hiroshima and Nagasaki were fission bombs of 12.5 kilotons (or 12,500 tons of TNT) and

22 kilotons respectively. A one-megaton thermonuclear bomb (the equivalent of one *million* tons of TNT), though an average-sized bomb by today's standards, is a full eighty times as powerful as the Hiroshima bomb was. Today, though larger bombs of 15, 20, and 25-megatons exist in the superpower arsenals, the following observations will be based upon the damage that has been recorded during the experimental detonation of one-megaton bombs.

When a 1-Mt. bomb is exploded at or immediately above ground level on a large city, its enormous destructive energy is delivered in several distinct forms.[1] The first thing noticeable from a distance is a silent, blinding, two-second flash with the brilliance of several suns. This pulse of ultraviolet radiation travels at the speed of light and will momentarily blind people within a radius of 13 miles on a clear day, and 53 miles on a clear night.

While people are rubbing their eyes in the distance, a great orange fireball of exploding gases is roaring outward from the thirty million degree core, vaporizing and melting everything in its mile-wide circle. This phenomenal heat that will melt concrete is called thermal radiation, and it accounts for about 35% of the total energy released by the bomb. During the first minute, its radiation behaves like sunlight: anything in a direct unshaded line is exposed and is subject to varying degrees of charring and burning; anything behind a wall, a tree, or even clothing, will be protected to some extent by shade. It is certain, however, that no unprotected person within a three-mile radius would survive its temperatures.

At seven miles, people outside would experience first-degree burns, the equivalent of a bad sunburn; at six miles they would receive second-degree burns, which blister and permanently scar the skin; and at five miles they would suffer third-degree burns, which permanently destroy skin tissue and require grafting. Of those who lived to endure such injuries, all who had received 25-30% of body surface burns in the second or third degrees would require intensive care in a hospital. It is estimated that as many as 75,000 people could thus survive a single bomb dropped on a large city. In the whole United States, however, there are only 2000 acute care burn beds. For most burn victims, death would follow a period of intense, unrelieved pain.

A far greater number would be killed outright, however, by the next burst of energy, a savage blast of air pressure called "overpressure", which is measured in pounds per square inch (psi), and whose first action would be to blow a crater 1000 feet wide and 200 feet deep at the point of explosion. The contents of the crater — usually skyscrapers and earth — would be partially vaporized by the roaring fireball, and then sucked through it into a massive rising cloud of radioactive soot and dust. Some of the contents would be deposited in a rim of radioactive soil, 2000 feet wide, around the crater. From this scene of apocalypse, a wall of compressed air — the blast wave — would surge outward at speeds exceeding 2000 miles per hour, flattening everything within a radius of 1.7 miles. Accompanying this blast wave, dragging, eddying winds would surround high buildings and topple them from their bases.

Further out, between 1.7 and 2.7 miles, the blast force would have dropped from 12 psi to 5 psi, and the winds to 160 mph. The 5 psi band is significant because, though still greater than hurricane force, it is the band in which people begin to survive: their bodies can withstand a 5 psi assault, whereas the walls of conventional houses cannot. In the 5-psi range, walls are blown out, windows explode, and cars are crushed or overturned. Fifty per cent of people in this area would be killed outright, most of them crushed by collapsing structures. Others would be hurled into walls, blown out of windows, or shredded by exploding glass and wood. Hardly anyone within this range would be left uninjured, and it is only when we reach the 2 psi band, from 2.7 to 4.7 miles radius, that we begin to find substantial numbers of people —

indoors — who would be intact. All those outside in a direct line with the blast would have been severely burned by thermal radiation.

The next major effect of an urban nuclear attack is the simultaneous ignition of thousands of fires. Close in, the thermal radiation flash spontaneously ignites (often through windows) combustibles such as newspapers, upholstered chairs, and clothing. Though most of these little fires are almost immediately extinguished by the succeeding blast wave, further out the blast wave starts fires which are then fanned by the winds: electrical fires, broken furnaces, exploding gas stations and fuel tanks, ruptured gas lines, and so on. When enough fuel exists, as in wood-frame residential neighborhoods, individual fires may coalesce into huge, 1000-square-mile firestorms — searing infernos of 800 degrees Centigrade. In its thirst for oxygen, such a fire would draw winds of 200 mph into its core, and around this fire people would either roast in their homes or their shelters, or asphyxiate from lack of air. Such fires may increase the lethal area of a bomb fivefold.

A second kind of mass fire is a conflagration, which is driven along a front by high winds, ever increasing in size as it consumes tires, running gasoline, fences, utility poles, houses, and bridges. An uninjured person may outrun such a fire on foot, but what of the injured, the handicapped, the elderly, and those who are attending wounded family and friends?

Survivors of these early minutes have not yet been exposed to lethal levels of radiation, because most of the fission fragments have been either deposited in the rim of the crater, or been hurled upwards at 300 mph within the ascending fireball. As the fireball rises it cools, causing strong upward "afterwinds" to suck soil and debris into the huge, purple, radioactive mushroom cloud. The stem of the mushroom is the updraft channel; swirling gases form the cap.

The cloud is made up of intensely radioactive fission products (the lighter atoms that resulted from fission), weapon fragments, water vapor, and pulverized debris. This mass of pulverized debris becomes uniformly contaminated by the fission particles and forms a huge lethal blanketing cloud. These dirty radioactive clouds are caused by ground-bursts only; air-bursts, though cleaner, inflict damage on much larger areas.

The cloud takes about ten minutes to form, and then remains visible for an hour or so before gradually dispersing to blend with the atmosphere. As the cloud cools, water droplets begin to condense around the contaminated particles, which become heavy and fall to earth in a pattern determined by the prevailing winds. If a steady southwest wind were blowing at 15 mph, a trailing, 30-mile wide cigar-shaped plume of fallout would form along a line to the northeast. The fallout from this radioactive plume would be so concentrated in the first 150 miles that anyone exposed to it for seven days would receive a cumulative dose of over 600 rems[2] of radiation, and would die within weeks. The next 100 miles along the plume would subject people to between 100 and 450 rems, causing them to become very sick and to recover in the short term, but inducing cancer and genetic damage in the long run.

The "prompt" or acute radiation emitted directly from the blast itself accounts for about 5% of the bomb's energy, but it does not reach beyond the range where rapid inevitable death would result from blast and fire. If, however, a person at one-mile radius had somehow managed to survive the blast effects, not even 24" of solid concrete could protect him from an immediate lethal dose of prompt radiation. And though there is a surprisingly small amount of prompt radiation further out, local "hot spots" may occur in random areas, where lethal exposures take place within hours.

A final and recently discovered direct effect of the bomb is the electromagnetic pulse (EMP), which is a sharp surge of voltage set in motion by fission. This sudden vicious burst of current rips through electrical circuits, shorting capacitors and burning out transistors. Lightning rods cannot respond in time to save equipment. One high altitude burst (125 miles up) from a moderately sized nuclear bomb would be enough to wipe out most solid-state circuitry in North America. This phenomenon has been christened "the chaos factor".[3] It raises serious questions concerning military communications during a "limited" nuclear war, and terrible questions regarding the aftermath awaiting survivors.

*　　　*　　　*

The mind is staggered by the devastation of a nuclear blast — by thirty million degrees of Centigrade — and turns off. But we must at all costs *succeed* in imagining it, so that our imagination will galvanize us with the will to avoid it. Every parent imagines with chilling accuracy the fate of a small child left untended in the street; now we must all imagine the fate of humanity left untended in the corridors of privilege and power.

Imagine yourself in a helicopter, flying into the smouldering heart of New York the day after it had been hit by a one-megaton bomb. You would not dare to land anywhere near the gaping radioactive crater at the blast site — which is all that would remain of nine city blocks of skyscrapers. All that you could see in any direction would be a flattened uniformity of scorched rubble dozens of feet deep, with the occasional twisted girder profiled against the sky. Downtown, you would have no sense of direction at all — no streets, street-signs, or landmarks. All identifiable objects: buses; taxis; trucks; the contents of office buildings, department stores, theaters, churches, and apartments — all would be crushed, melted and charred, as would be the roughly-shaped remains of hundreds of thousands of human and animal corpses. What yesterday had been a bustling, prosperous, historical giant of a city would today be a profound silence.

42

A Visit to Armageddon

Your spirit would open to an immense and unforgettable sorrow.

As you circled outwards in your helicopter, you would begin to recognize the upright skeletal remains of buildings. About four miles out, there would be room on a wide street, among the wrecked cars, splintered power poles, shingles, bricks, and shards of glass, to set down the helicopter and step out. From within the semi-collapsed houses you would begin to hear the moans and cries of an overwhelming human misery — the wretchedness of the burned, the crushed, the dying, and the blind. The wails of lost and panicked children. The utter helplessness of the newborn, the sick, the disabled, and the elderly.

For miles in every direction the wounded would be trapped where they lay, without heat, water, or electricity. If it were a winter night, the cold and darkness would have compounded the toll. People would not be sure what had hit them.

In Hiroshima, which in 1945 was a city of 245,000 people, many were able to walk, in a kind of dazed, catatonic state, away from the city. But in a larger city, the word "trapped" would take on a special meaning. No car would be driveable, nor any street passable, within a four or five mile radius of the blast. How many injured people would be able to clear their way out of central Chicago, Los Angeles, Montreal, or London? And if they could, where would they go?

It hardly bears thinking about, being trapped in an area where two-thirds of the people were dead, and nearly all of the remainder injured: within days, especially in summer, the decomposition of the dead, and the vomiting and defecation of the living would produce a nightmare of intolerable, sickening stench. Not to mention the flies, the heat, the prowling dogs and cats, and the inevitable birds of prey.

If the bomb on New York had been a 25-megaton bomb — and there are many, and they are so immensely destructive that their only logical application can be the obliteration of a large city — then the 5-psi conditions would extend for a radius of ten miles.

43

And if 30% of the population in that area (80 or 90 square miles) were alive and immobilized, then hundreds of thousands of agonized people would be waiting for a help which could never come after an all-out nuclear war.

But to be *really* serious about leveling New York, the city would have to be divided into a number of 25-Mt. quadrants, and of course we do know that there are enough weapons to do this. Not only to New York, but to all American cities, all Canadian cities, all British, French, and West German cities. But of course they would never do it, because we would do it right back . . .

CHAPTER 5

A MIDDLE-SIZED WAR:
Synopsis of Effects

1. *Health Effects and Medical Shortcomings*

Many worried medical and public health professionals have been striving to alert the public to the realities of a nuclear aftermath. They urge people to understand that nuclear war is *not* survivable; that the health care system would not be able to offer even the most basic medical assistance: drug relief from pain. Health authorities condemn as unethical the false hopes which are raised in the public mind by civil defense and relocation plans, plans which are not only costly in themselves, but which divert money and attention away from the only feasible approach to the problem, the *prevention* of nuclear war.

First, they warn, because hospitals are located in prime-target (urban) areas, they and their personnel would be destroyed at a higher rate than the general population. In Hiroshima, for example, only 3 of 45 hospitals were unaffected; 65 of 150 doctors were killed outright and most of the remainder injured; and of 1780 nurses, only 126 were able to assist. And remember that Hiroshima's trauma was inflicted by a small, crude uranium bomb, exploding high enough to prevent ground-burst radiation fall-out. The following is an account of one of the surviving physicians:

> "Dr. Sasaki worked without method, taking those who were nearest to him first, and he noticed soon that the corridor seemed to be getting more and more crowded. Mixed in with

the abrasions and lacerations which most people in the hospital had suffered, he began to find dreadful burns. He realized then that casualties were pouring in from outdoors. There were so many that he began to pass up the lightly wounded; he decided that all he could hope to do was to stop people from bleeding to death. Before long, patients lay and crouched on the floors of the wards and the laboratories and all other rooms, and in the corridors, and on the stairs, and in the front hall, and under the porte cochere, and on the stone front steps, and in the driveway and courtyard, and for blocks each way in the streets outside. Wounded people supported maimed people; disfigured families leaned together. Many people were vomiting. A tremendous number of schoolgirls — some of those who had been taken from their classrooms to work outdoors clearing fire lanes — crept into the hospital. The people in the suffocating crowd inside the hospital wept and cried, for Dr. Sasaki to hear, "Sensei! Doctor!" and the less seriously wounded came and pulled at his sleeve and begged him to go to the aid of the worse wounded. Tugged here and there in his stockinged feet, bewildered by the numbers, staggered by so much raw flesh, Dr. Sasaki lost all sense of profession and stopped working as a skillful surgeon and a sympathetic man; he became an automaton, mechanically wiping, daubing, winding, wiping, daubing, winding."[1]

The Health Commissioner of Philadelphia recently estimates that if a one-megaton bomb were dropped on that city, there would be 800 wounded people waiting for each remaining hospital bed.[2]

An optimistic calculation[3] of the patient-doctor ratio following a modern-day nuclear attack on a major city estimates approximately 1700 acutely injured persons for each functioning doctor. If each physician worked for 20 hours a day, it would take eight days to see each of 1,000 patients once for only ten minutes. In the absence of hospital facilities, medical supplies, blood transfusions, and nursing support, one ten-minute visit would be hopelessly inadequate to treat the massive burns, shock, hemorrhage, organ ruptures and acute radiation sickness that would abound.

A model[4] of the expected consequences of a 6,559-megaton nuclear attack on the USA has been prepared by the Federal Emergency Management Agency for defense planning purposes. The energy yield would be equivalent to 524,720 Hiroshimas. Targets in the model include military installations, industrial and transportation facilities, plus a 4000-megaton distribution upon cities of 50,000 or more population.

Within moments of such an attack, an estimated 86 million people (40% of the population) would be dead, and 34 million (27% of the survivors) would be severely injured. An additional 50 million deaths are expected to occur within the following few weeks known as the "shelter period", in which radioactive levels would require survivors to remain underground. Only 60 million people (28% of the original total) are expected to live through the initial barrage and shelter periods to face the post-shelter aftermath and the final so-called recovery period. Each survivor could look forward to renewing acquaintances with at least 28% of his old friends, once "recovery" had been completed. Some survivalists, who tolerate the idea of nuclear war, actually claim to be eager for a holocaust, sensing that they would survive while certain less desirable elements of the population would not.[5]

The shelter period, which lasts from day one to the end of the first month, is fraught with obstacles. Initially, many sheltering in the blast and firestorm vicinities would succumb to suffocation, smoke inhalation, and heat prostration. Others, with burns and blast injuries, would die unaided by medicine.

People would have received varying doses of radiation, but they would have no idea how much. The body has no evolutionary experience of such radiation levels, and therefore is totally defenseless against them. Biological processes are organized at the cellular level, which is huge compared to the tiny, high-velocity rays and particles of nuclear fission. At extremely high exposures (5000 rems or more) convulsions from central nervous system damage lead quickly to death. At sudden exposure to 450-600 rems, cell membranes are percolated by these sub-atomic fission bullets, and blood vessels begin to leak into the brain and lungs. The stomach and intestines become raw and ulcerated, causing rapid loss of blood and body fluids, diarrhea, massive intestinal infection, high fever, and death.

Where sub-lethal exposures occur (100-400 rems), symptoms developing over a period of weeks include vomiting, hair loss, bruising, diarrhea, and infection. Though recovery from these levels usually occurs, the radiation sickness lowers the body's resistance to disease, a deadly complication to the infections resulting from burns.

Those dependent upon insulin, digitalis, cortisone, and a host of other medicines would succumb to what had been a previously-manageable infirmity. Persons with pacemakers would be literally short-circuited by the electromagnetic pulse. And a universal blanket of psychological shock, whose nausea and vomiting mimic the symptoms of acute radiation sickness, would demoralize even the unexposed with the false expectation of impending death.

Undesirable shelter conditions, such as crowding, extremes of temperature, poor sanitation, and lack of food, water, and fuel would tax even the strongest. In hot shelters, an adult requires one gallon of water per day to prevent dehydration. And though previously healthy adults can tolerate a period of food scarcity, children readily suffer malnutrition.

The fate of the thousands trapped in large public shelters would be much worse. Heat and humidity, lack of food and water, and the force of numbers would produce epidemic hepatitis, intestinal infections, and respiratory diseases. Amidst shock, rivalry, and disorientation, the living would have to care for the sick, cope with the dying, and somehow dispose of the dead.

After a month of this gruelling hibernation, about half the people who had reached "shelter" would blinkingly emerge, in a weakened depressed state to survey the waiting rabble of landscape, smelling of death and alive with the buzzing of flies and insects.

The post-shelter period can be imagined as a public health monstrosity unparalleled in history by even the worst conditions of plague-ridden Europe. Dr. Howard Hiatt, former Dean of the Harvard School of Public Health, has described nuclear war as "the greatest public health hazard of all time." A computer simulation[6] of a one-megaton attack near a single large city estimated that in the absence of medical intervention, 35% of the survivors would die from infectious diseases alone within the first year after the attack. And modern medical intervention would hardly exist, for it is technologically dependent upon an intact and functioning social fabric — for all of its hospitals, laboratories, diagnostic equipment, surgical procedures, and antibiotics. We no longer have the medical, cultural or social survival skills to be plunged into a technology-deficient third-world type of cataclysm. People would die like flies from the old scourges which have been largely eliminated from modern societies: cholera, typhoid, malaria, plague, yellow fever, typhus, and tuberculosis. With most medical laboratories and pharmaceutical suppliers located in high-risk areas, the surviving physicians would be forced to squander scarce and precious antibiotics on the unverified diagnoses of diseases they had hitherto not seen in America.

In addition, basic public health conditions that we have long taken for granted — a clean water supply, a sewage system, and unending supplies of inspected refrigerated food — would suddenly be luxuries of the past, with epidemics from the history books surfacing to haunt the present.

Most humans, animals, and birds would be dead. Resistant to radiation, and in their place, would be an explosion of flies, mosquitoes, and countless other insects, with few birds to keep them in check. Insecticide stocks would be grossly inadequate to meet these flourishing insect populations with their attendant malaria, typhus, dengue, and encephalitis. Most surviving animals would have suffered radiation exposure and with it susceptibility to brucellosis, leptospirosis, and rabies, all of which may be transmitted to man.

Economic conditions would magnify the toll on health. The transformed post-nuclear world would be desperately short of food, housing, clothing, and fuel. And a long period of sustained labor, poor nutrition, and exposure to the elements would lead to exhaustion and despair.

And how long would it take exhausted men and women to erase the ugliness of this man-made slag-heap? Could they even imagine a time when the sparkling natural beauty of the earth would be restored? In the Hiroshima experience they could not:

> "The kind of terror experienced by survivors can be understood from the rumors that quickly spread among them. One rumor simply held that everyone in Hiroshima would be dead within a few months or a few years. The symbolic message here was: None can escape the poison; the epidemic is total — all shall die. But there was a second rumor, reported to me even more frequently and with greater emotion: the belief that trees, grass, and flowers would never again grow in Hiroshima; that from that day the city would be unable to sustain vegetation of any kind. The meaning here was that nature was drying up altogether. Life was being extinguished at its source — an ultimate form of desolation that not only encompassed human death but went beyond it."[7]

It is under such circumstances that human beings lose their love for life and their will to live. They sit down in a quiet place and wait to die.

2. *Long-Term Climatic Effects*

The foregoing medical and public health consequences of nuclear war illustrate the direct short-term effects on people close to areas of attack. Recent estimates,[8] based on a 5,000-10,000 megaton war, predict that these direct effects would extend to: a) 750 million people who would be killed outright by the blast; b) a further 1.1 billion who would die soon after from the combined effects of blast, fire, and radiation; and c) a still further 1.1 billion with injuries requiring medical attention. These are conservative estimates, based upon a moderate fraction of existing arsenals, and do not allow for the greatly expanded arsenals that are planned for the later eighties. So at least 30-50% of the world's population, mostly in the Northern hemisphere, is apt to be directly and immediately involved.

What, then, of the two or three billion post-war survivors? Recent discoveries suggest that the long-term global effects of atmospheric dust and smoke may be as devastating to humans as the immediate, local effects.

We have seen that millions of tons of particles would be explosively ejected from bomb craters into the upper atmosphere. In addition, the soot and smoke from countless fires — in cities, forests, shrublands, oilfields, and storage tanks — would rage aloft. In a 10,000-Mt. war, this high blanket of black cloud would absorb up to 99% of the sun's light,[9] heating the upper atmosphere while cooling the earth. Mid-continental temperatures would be expected to plummet to $-40°$ Centigrade for many weeks, taking a year to return to normal. And radiation levels averaging 500 rads would quickly cover 30% of Northern hemisphere lands.

The Southern hemisphere is not expected to do much better: light would be reduced to 10% of normal, and temperatures to $-18°C$. Tropical plants are temperature-fragile, and it is known from experience that they are devastated by even cool temperature pulses. These broad-leafed jungles play a crucial role in the evaporation of the world's fresh water, and their absence or reduction would lead to a sluggish rain cycle, which in turn would imperil the world's vegetation.

Another far-reaching disturbance is the expected depletion of the atmospheric ozone layer by nitrogen oxides released from the explosions. Part of the sun's ultraviolet radiation, known as UV-B, has a very high wavelength which is biologically damaging to plant and animal cells. There is enough of this UV-B in ordinary sunlight to cause skin cancer in some people, and to reduce the body's immunity to infection in others. The ozonosphere presently offers the earth a protective shield against this part of the ultraviolet spectrum by selectively absorbing it as it passes through. But a 5,000-Mt. war would double the existing UV-B, and 10,000 megatons would quadruple it. As only minor additional doses of UV-B are weakening to plant leaves and human immune systems, the results of such gross multiplications could be disastrous.

The ecological effects of these combined climatic disruptions would be vast, interconnected, and unpredictable. Even little "El Nino", a mildly warming ocean current along the Pacific Coast, has produced alarming effects, including the die-off of certain vulnerable commercial fish and seafoods.

Plants, for example, which require at least 20% of existing light levels to carry on photosynthesis and to grow, would weaken and die from light loss alone. The combined effects of reduced light, radiation, freezing temperatures, and increased UV-B make it difficult to imagine that they could survive at all.

Some plants and trees (notably evergreens) are particularly sensitive to ionizing radiation, and would die at exposures to 500-1,000 rems, as would all human beings and animals in the 30% of the continent which would receive such doses. These dead forests would burn like tinder, producing advanced soil erosion and large tracts of desert. Such deserts could sustain only the most tenacious and undemanding of grasses, which in turn would offer the minimum of moisture and nourishment to man and beast alike. What vegetation did survive would be at the mercy of an uncontrolled explosion of parasitic insects, whose biological systems are curiously resistant to the effects of radiation.

Regional temperature differences are expected to generate strong winds, and with them dust storms and further erosion. The coasts, with temperatures moderated by the relative warmth of ocean waters, would suck high pressure winds from the frigid inland continent. In turn, these winds would fan tidal waves, which would splinter ports, marinas, fish-boats, and barges. Coastal commerce would be further decimated by the UV-B toll on surface marine plankton, which in slowing the food chain would play havoc with the fisheries.

The upper atmosphere (or stratosphere), heated by dust and soot, would reverse the natural order by becoming warmer than the lower atmosphere (or troposphere). The resulting wind currents and airstream changes would spread the dust and soot to the remotest corners of the planet, making most of the world's countries captive to the fallout from somebody else's war. The art of computerized scenario development is simply not up to modeling all the possible changes that might occur in wind and ocean currents, and their untold effects on world climate.

A further insult to survivors would be unprecedented levels of airborne chemicals. During the great urban firestorms, the widespread combustion of synthetic materials would pour out deadly compounds such as dioxins for perennial circulation in the atmosphere.

The foregoing interdependent climatic effects are but a few threads in what would amount to a universally torn and disrupted ecological fabric — a fabric that has taken millions of years to weave into a beautiful, intricate, and harmonious natural balance. Are we, in a late twentieth-century dispute over transient economic systems, so self-important in our perspective, and stubborn in our ways, as to push this risk of holocaust to the point of doom? A risk whose actualization may negate not only the whole of Earth's evolution to the present, but its vast unseen possibilities for the future?

3. *Agricultural Effects*

Even without this dramatic ecological shake-up, agriculture would be in serious trouble. We tend to think of agriculture as being "out on the farm", but many of its essential components — seeds, fertilizers, pesticides, fuel, and farm equipment — are stored in and distributed from cities, which are at high risk for bombing. If war were to come in winter or early spring, the sowing of crops would be all but eliminated.

If war were to come in summer or early fall, harvesting without fuel would require animal and human labor, yet surviving farm animals would be far more in demand for butchering than for work. Even if a reasonable harvest could be reaped, post-attack transportation systems would be too shattered to distribute the food. This in turn would force the migration of urban survivors to the countryside in search of food, water and shelter. There, faced with third-world soil and economic conditions, but lacking third-world agricultural skills, survivors would eke out a subsistence on grains and meats that would be contaminated with radioactivity for years to come.

The Northern Hemisphere would not be the only victim of a ravished agriculture. Many aid-dependent developing countries have been responding to imports of wheat, fuel, and fertilizer with a corresponding population growth. An abrupt severance of this agricultural assistance would plunge these onlooking countries into a state of famine, disease, and social unrest worse than any they had previously conquered. Efforts to compensate these imports through domestic agriculture would be drastically curtailed by droughts and untold other aberrations of a rearranged world ecology. So though in North America and the Soviet Union a population loss might roughly match a depleted agriculture, much of the third world would face mass starvation.

A Middle-Sized War

4. *Economic Effects*

At the heart of capitalism is the fundamental fact that if the economy does not continue to grow, it will collapse. The system is based upon profits (savings left over after essential life needs have been met) being invested back into businesses, which in turn must grow and make profits to justify the investments made in them.

Nuclear weapons threaten this system in two fundamental ways. First, the arms race costs the United States a great deal more than can be raised by taxation alone. The U.S. Government is forced, therefore, to borrow billions of saved dollars from the American public, which it does by selling bonds. In the meantime, ordinary businesses are also trying to borrow money from the general public, through the banking intermediary. There is thus a competition going on between the Federal Government and ordinary businesses for the available savings of the nation. But whereas business can and will go under if it does not show a profit (which means that there is a limit to the interest rates it can afford to pay on loans), governments hardly ever go under, because they do not live and die by the rules of capitalism. So in the borrowing competition for available saved dollars, the Government wins hands down: it simply bids whatever interest rates are needed to beat business out of the contest, amassing further debt as it goes along. This, very simply, is how the arms race has been fueling interest rates, depriving business of affordable loans, and ultimately depressing the entire economy. In this ultimate sense, the cold war is an economic conflict to determine which side can better withstand and maintain the economic hardship imposed by arms racing. This economic strain is the first way that the weapons undermine capitalism, which (a terrible irony) they are built to protect.

The second way is by war iself. In the strife following a nuclear attack, the idea of savings would be completely eliminated, as all the available production and energy would be channeled into the basics of food, clothing, shelter, and medical care. These essentials would not be met by a surviving industrial base. The first objective of war is to cripple the enemy's fighting ability, so prime targets are economic as well as military, and include electrical, oil, gas, and transportation facilities. Once these have been hit, any remaining equipment or industry becomes quite useless. "To illustrate the vulnerability of the economy in a nuclear war, two one-megaton warheads would destroy the Baytown refinery in Baytown, Texas, which supplies approximately 3.5 percent of the total U.S. oil-refining capacity. Eighty one-megaton warheads would destroy 64 percent of the total refining capacity for the country. Similarly, 64 40-kiloton and nine 170-kiloton warheads would destroy 73 percent of the total USSR petroleum-refining capacity." [10]

Shattered transportation, communication and electrical networks would make banking impossible, and money would become meaningless as a medium for exchange. In its place there would be a return to simple trading — the bartering of the Middle Ages that exists in certain primitive societies even today. It is ironic that under such primitive economic conditions, neither capitalism nor communism, both of which require an industrial base, would have any further relevance.

The failure of money, banking, and transportation would spell the end of international trade and commerce for years to come, with unimaginable consequences for countries specializing in a narrow range of exports.

In conclusion, we see that the over 800,000 annual millions which are spent worldwide on defense are a major factor in the inflation and weakened economies which in turn produce the tensions that lead to war. "Thus the very arms race that begins as an alleged effort to protect a way of life has as its likely consequences the loss of those freedoms and opportunities we seek to preserve."[11] In spite of this self-defeating contradiction — which could be understood in grade school — both sides persist in amassing the tools of war. Every American, indeed every free Westerner who stands by and endures this treacherous contradiction, is, in the final analysis, lending his implicit support to it.

5. *Social and Psychological Effects*

As with the economic effects, the social and psychological effects may be divided into those which result from the *threat* of nuclear war, and those which would result from war itself.

It is more than 40 years that the lurking potential for planetary ruin has been brooding above the unconscious mind of the modern world. This big "but" has been hanging over the world, and, like a dark cloud which overshadows the sun, the nuclear presence has weighed heavily on the spirit of human happiness.

There may be no better indicator of a culture's mood and awareness than the contemporary popular music of the day. Most of the impetus for the music of any day comes from youth in love, but through this music also comes the characteristic energy and feeling of the times. Thus we have the "roaring twenties", the blues and jazz from the thirties, the big band sound and sentimental crooning from the forties, the rock and roll from the fifties, the soul-searching lamentations of the sixties, and so on.

It is particularly revealing to look at twentieth-century American popular music from the cut-off between the prenuclear and postnuclear age.

The pre-1945 music expressed many moods — it was lively, or sentimental, or blue, or hopelessly romantic, or just plain silly. It was folksy, fun, and sometimes sublime, but across all these moods it maintained a kind of superficiality or innocence that has largely disappeared.

The intent of music seemed to change when the first generation that was born under the nuclear threat came of age. The children of the forties were the song-writers of the sixties, and they were *depressed.* The music of the sixties was suddenly a social and political raising of consciousness. Through such artists as Bob Dylan, Joan Baez, Peter, Paul and Mary, and Simon and Garfunkel, American youth focused its sorrow upon a violent and injust world, a world of racial tensions, social injustices, and interpersonal conflicts that suddenly *mattered.* The Viet Nam nonwar forced a cynical coming of age on what had been an innocent, adolescent America. Since then, the direction that music has taken has been anything but happy, with rock and punk groups parodying the cynicism of the age with their own names: The Police, The Stranglers, The Killing Joke, The Anarchy, The Styx, The Twisted Sister, and so on.

This trend to incorporate the violence and the bizarre into music did not just materialize out of thin air. Far more likely it is an expression of hopelessness, hurled out by youth through its music. The now middle-aged adults, the great revolutionary flower-generation from the sixties, has let the side down and their own children with it by allowing the proliferation of the bomb to rage out of control under their mid-life auspices.

Viet Nam was the apparent key to the anti-establishment protest, as seen in the drugs, the hard rock, the long hair, the opting-out dress, and the communes. But Viet Nam would not have been attempted if America the bully had not been far enough ahead in the 1960's, as we shall see later, to work nuclear blackmail upon the Soviet Union. This was not a defensive war in any sense, and with it, and with the huge muscle of nuclear strength that lurked behind it, began the ugliness that has fundamentally changed the way that Americans feel about themselves. There has been a loss in the culture's lightness and innocence; people are openly, stoically carrying a guilt that is almost visible. It is the stain of knowing that our great, rich, promised land is using its nuclear might to squeeze the world in its grip. It is the guilt and isolation of the bully, who in turning against any part of mankind is turning ultimately against himself, and is coarsening his own fragility and sensitivity in the process. This is a deadening process, in which the investment of self in unconditional childlike happiness becomes frozen at its source.

How is the nuclear age affecting the psychology of America in general? Scarcely a day goes by when the cultural preoccupation with nuclear war is not somewhere in the news. The resulting sense that there may be no tomorrow makes everything vaguely provisional. It seems futile to sacrifice present energies to a future which may never come, so there is a tendency to "live and be merry, for tomorrow we die". In vulnerable people, particularly the young, feelings of hopelessness and powerlessness may actually lead to depression and withdrawal from reality. It is probably no accident, therefore, that America's divorce rates, child and adolescent suicides, and drug and alcohol rates have never been higher than they are today.

Though the literature of psychology has been late to address the impact of nuclearism, one thing is certain, and that is that society has not evolved towards stability and permanence during the nuclear age. How much determination can there be to hold a family together, for the sake of the children, when the world may be in ashes tomorrow, and the children may never grow up?

Children have been more a topic of the literature than have adults. They cannot flee from their fears into the adult defense mechanisms that permit business as usual. They awake in terror from nightmares of holocaust; they talk about not growing up; they cannot fathom how we adults have brought them into a world in which we cannot protect them from *our* activities. This bewilderment at our lack of care and concern mystifies them to the roots of their beings, and they turn away in bitterness to erase the pain of our frozen response. In what other age have *children* committed suicide? May God help us for not helping them.

Let us turn now to the social and psychological effects of nuclear war itself. Here, general observations of mass catastrophe point to three kinds of behavioral changes in survivors.[12] First, they experience a profound apathy, a feeling that the world is finished and that there is no sense in doing anything. Second, they become lost and disoriented, unable to get a meaningful fix on their location in time and space — unable to remember the names of streets and friends. Third, they lose the feeling of being connected to other people, and enter a private world of isolation and loneliness. It has been estimated[13] that about one-third of the survivors would suffer from pronounced anxiety reactions such as fear, apprehensiveness, irritability, and confusion.

In Hiroshima, many people adapted to the overwhelming emotional stress of the disaster by retreating into a psychic closing-off state which lasted from hours to days and even months, merging finally into long-term feelings of depression and despair. Others developed the "disaster syndrome", an apathy resulting from the sudden loss of confidence in the safety of life. There is an almost universal need in human beings to forget that they are going to die, and when this needed sense is violently disputed by an overwhelming catastrophe, confidence is displaced by futility and depression.

Many Hiroshima survivors developed the "atomic bomb neurosis", a feeling that their health and the health of their children was under, and would always be under, a shadow of doubt. Such people often suffered chronic hypochrondria, characterized by weakness, nervousness, fatigue, susceptibility to colds and stomach ailments, and so on. In this way the emotional impact of the explosions proved to be a life-long encounter, with no escape or resolution. These persistent after-effects seem to be unique to nuclear disasters.

In Japan the victims of the bombs are known as "Hibakusha", and are generally regarded as bearing the taint of death. They find it difficult to marry and gain employment, and have a sense of being handicapped — of being outcasts. At the time, these survivors experienced a terrible guilt for continuing to live in the midst of so much agonizing death. In the words of Dr. Lifton:

> "For survivors seem not only to have experienced the atomic disaster, but to have imbibed it and incorporated it into their being, including all of its elements of horror, evil, and particularly of death. They feel compelled virtually to merge with those who died, not only with close family members but with a more anonymous group of 'the dead' . . . . The special quality of guilt over surviving takes shape through the following inner sequence: I almost died; I should have died; I did die, or at least am not really alive; if I am live, it is impure of me to be so; and anything that I do that affirms life is also impure and an insult to the dead, who alone are pure.[14]

In Hiroshima the "psychic numbing" state, or emotional retreat, often involved behaviors which violated very strong cultural traditions and taboos. In the absence of police intervention and psychiatric support, the anti-social behavior of thousands, if not millions of disturbed people would become one of the most difficult and dangerous problems of post-attack society.

The social implications of nuclear war are endless. The destruction of cities would include the destruction of vital records such as land registration, and with them the security for ownership, tenancy, and inheritance. In a land full of dispossessed, frightened people, chaos and desperation would lead to civil violence, repressive vigilante groups, and a general nihilism based on the sense of having nothing to lose. And haunting everyone would be the knowledge that when they had it good, they weren't smart enough to keep it; most of them hadn't even tried.

Chapter 6

THE CIVIL DEFENSE FRAUD:
A Dangerous and Costly Illusion

As we observed in the last chapter, the health, economical, social, and ecological consequences of a nuclear war do not permit any meaningful concept of defense, once its unfathomable destructive force has been unleashed upon the world. Why then, is there any serious talk about "civil defense"?

A large part of the answer lies in our traditional expectations of civil defense, which rises to the occasion during natural disasters such as floods, earthquakes, hurricanes, and forest fires. In addition, the original nuclear arsenals were made up of small numbers of inaccurate atomic bombs, deliverable by carrier-based bombers. In those early days, conventional air defense, evacuation of cities, and air-raid shelters were still feasible responses to atomic attack. There was more time to react (today we have 30 minutes), and the old atom bombs were only one-eightieth as devastating as the new hydrogen ones.

Though there have been a few brief flurries of American public concern over civil defense (e.g., after the Soviets exploded their first atomic bomb in 1949; after "Sputnik" was launched in 1957; and following the Cuban Missile Crisis of 1962), Congress has, in the main, refused to substantially fund it. The view has prevailed that defense sheltering is neither practical nor cost-effective in terms of the extreme destructive power of nuclear weapons. The advantages of building expensive shelters could be easily overcome by intensifying the attack, which is a far cheaper thing to do than build shelters. The result has been an ever-growing lead in offensive over defensive technology.

In the Antiballistic Missile (ABM) Treaty of 1972, the Soviets and Americans mutually recognized the futility of pursuing defense technology by limiting ABM sites on both sides to two. In 1976, the United States closed down the one ABM site that it did develop.

This early freedom from concern over civil defense was founded, until the mid 1970's, upon American confidence in the doctrine of deterrence. This doctrine (which will be considered at greater length in Chapter 7) assumes, very simply, that neither side would be tempted to attack the other if it knew that it would be annihilated in return. This principle came to be known under Robert McNamara as mutual assured destruction (MAD), and as long as it was trusted, civil defense remained largely irrelevant.

In 1976, however, after a five-year period of reduced surveillance in the USSR, U.S. intelligence was alarmed to discover a considerable growth in Soviet protection programs. Panic spread as the word went out that the American arsenal was no longer capable of penetrating Soviet civil defenses; deterrence had been thrown off balance, and the USSR was now in a position to launch a successful first strike. A cry emerged for a full-scale increase in accurate offensive weaponry.

Thinking about a failed deterrence meant thinking about war itself — about fighting nuclear war and about defending the country from its effects. Attention swung from preventing the apocalypse to fighting it and limiting it once it had inevitably begun. Common sense had yielded to panic.

Having accepted the possibility of war, strategists began to increase its likelihood by actually planning its course. This new emphasis on war-fighting superiority displaced in many minds the old appreciation for the actual dimensions of nuclear war — for the mile-wide craters and the thirty-million degree concrete-vaporizing blasts. As T.K. Jones, the Deputy Undersecretary of Defense for Strategic and Nuclear Forces assured the nation in

1982, "everybody's going to make it if there are enough shovels to go around . . . . Dig a hole, cover it with a couple of doors and then throw three feet of dirt on top. It's the dirt tht does it."[1]

To help everybody make it, the Federal Emergency Management Agency (FEMA) had already begun work on a crisis relocation plan based upon a 6,000-10,000 megaton attack scenario. (It was still not considered feasible to fortify the cities with the concrete casings of blast shelters.)

FEMA made two basic assumptions; first, that if the Soviets were to resort to attack during an international crisis, they would attempt to destroy the major military installations and industrial plants of the United States. There were about 250 cities of over 50,000 people (a total of 145 million) located within the blast ranges of these expected targets. Before initiating an attack, went the second assumption, the Soviets would gear up their own civil defense plans to meet the resulting counter-attack. This meant that the U.S. satellite intelligence system would be able to detect the Soviet's own evacuation of people from target areas, which in requiring three to five days would provide ample advance warning of an impending attack.

At this point the U.S. Government would begin to notify its citizens of their respective safety destinations and traffic routes. One hundred and forty-five million people would take to the road, heading out in unknown weather conditions to shelter with friends in the country, or to report to rural camps which would be stockpiled with food and supplies. Here they would build their own fallout shelters before the Soviet attack.[2] However, government fallout shelters are not expected to be in place until the late 1990's,[3] by which time the American demographic patterns will have so shifted as to make the current plan obsolete.

There has been considerable speculation regarding the public health problems of the evacuation itself.[4] These would include stress-induced increases in seizures, insulin reactions, strokes, respiratory and cardiac arrests, depressive reactions, and intestinal bleeding. The situation would be compounded by the special needs of the pregnant, newborn, aged, handicapped, and chronically ill. Another unknown factor is the amount of violence and crime that would be triggered, with survival mechanisms operating at peak force, by traffic congestion, fear of the unknown, and police preoccupation with the logistics of the relocation.

Dr. Eric Chivian, a psychiatrist at M.I.T., has described civil defense plans as dangerous because they create the illusion that we can survive a nuclear war. He has identified[5] ten underlying assumptions to the crisis relocation plan, and has disqualified each one in turn:

1) that the build-up of tensions would be sufficiently gradual to permit time for evacuation to take place. This does not allow for a sudden escalation in conflict, a flash preemptive Soviet strike, or an accidental release of warheads.

2) that it will be possible to recognize the critical time in the crisis when evacuation should be ordered. Evacuation on either side would not only disrupt the economy (which is the enemy's objective to do), but it would signal the possible intention of that side to be preparing for attack itself. Evacuation is therefore a preliminary step towards war which both sides are reluctant to take.

3) that the relocation would be heard, obeyed, and carried out in an orderly way. Many people would be beyond media communication, some would panic, and others would resist the order or have alternative plans for themselves.

4) that it would be possible to orderly evacuate a large city under wartime conditions at all. Sheer numbers, panic, no truly safe destination, inadequate escape routes, and lack of private transportation would all add to confusion and resistance.

5) that Soviet missiles would not be retargeted after the evacuation. As the purpose of strategic attack includes the destruction of populations as well as industrial facilities, and as retargeting can

be done within minutes, it is possible that these migrant populations might be virtually followed by bombs.

6) that is it possible to predict"safe" areas in advance. This is quite unrealistic, given the pervasive nature of radiation fallout.

7) that shelters can provide adequate protection from fallout. Even if relatively "safe" areas were reached, protection would still be needed, and there would not be enough large, ventilated, radiation-proof shelters for the vast numbers of transient people.

8) that basic survival needs will be met in shelters. These include food, water, air, sanitation, energy, and medical supplies, and will be required to last large numbers of sick and distraught people for long periods of time — up to 30 days where initial fallout levels are 1000 rems, and up to 100 days where levels reach 3000 rems.

9) that after a week or two people will emerge to rebuild society. Outdoor radiation levels are not expected to be safe for weeks or months. Psychiatrists predict that after this amount of time survivors will be so shocked and disoriented that they will not have the physical or psychological strength to start again.

10) that systems will be in place to rebuild society. The complex food, energy, transportation, and delivery systems of our continental society would be shattered by a nuclear war. Because man's love for life is largely social, with the social fabric destroyed survival itself would have little meaning.

The City of Cambridge, Massachusetts, has declared civil defense measures to be futile, and has issued a public information pamphlet which states that "the sole means of protecting Cambridge citizens from nuclear warfare would be for nations with nuclear arms to destroy these arms and renounce their use."[6]

In April 1982, Stuart Shapiro, Health Commissioner for the City of Philadelphia, testified:

> "The consequences of nuclear war are so grave — just like cancer — that the only wise policy is one of prevention. The

health system of this great city would be destroyed by nuclear attack.

"It is my judgement that *any* support of any nuclear war crisis relocation plans would be inconsistent with my job as Health Commissioner and the duties and responsibilities of the Department of Public Health as outlined in the city charter.

"As Commissioner of Health of Philadelphia I come here to state clearly and directly that there is no way, no plan, no gimmick, no illusions about protecting health during a nuclear war. It cannot be done."[7]

*   *   *

Until now we have been dealing with "passive" defenses, (or "passive" damage limitation) — those which seek protection against warheads which have already arrived at their targets. As the United States has obviously not found them to be an attractive option for itself, why should the appearance of blast shelters and hardened industrial and military targets in the Soviet Union be thought to undermine deterrence? As one arms control expert has observed, "The recommendation against American passive defense programs was not merely the cost-avoiding (relatively speaking) course; it helped to define the problem in a way that favored the preferred solution of the military services and of the American defense industry; i.e., new or additional strategic offensive weapons . . . . The real concern of American military planners should be to avoid giving Soviet non-military passive defenses more public credit than they deserve, lest the Soviets place an unwarranted faith in them and err in their own strategic calculus. At the same time, the United States needs to avoid putting the Soviets in desperate situations where a growing threat to its retaliatory forces might make early initiation of a nuclear war seem the lesser of two evils."[8]

The act of "putting the Soviets in desperate situations" is called in military jargon "destabilizing". This brings us to the subject of "active" damage limitation, but first a word of introduction.

In contrast to passive damage limitation, active damage limitation seeks to destroy nuclear weapons on their way in. As we already know, the superpowers found it to their mutual advantage to sign the ABM Treaty of 1972, which virtually dead-ended the growth of antiballistic missiles. ABM's were not only expensive, but destabilizing to the offensive equation of deterrence. They would have forced the adversaries to mutually develop more powerful and accurate offensive missiles, which in gaining the capability to penetrate each other's defenses would have spawned even more sophisticated intercepting ABM's, and so ad infinitum. For the leaders of 1972, the writing was quite plainly on the wall.

In March, 1983, however, President Reagan called for an intensive and comprehensive effort to define a long-term research program with the ultimate goal of eliminating the threat posed by nuclear missiles. He sought to provide the defensive means of rendering these weapons impotent and obsolete. This ambition, morally solemnized by the President as a quest "to save lives rather than to avenge them", is known as the Strategic Defense Initiative (SDI), and more popularly as "Star Wars".

In President Reagan's mind, rendering the Soviet nuclear arsenal ineffectual in this way would make the world a safer place to live. The Soviets cannot be expected to share this view, however, for if the American objective were attained, there would be no effective Soviet counter to an American first strike. The Russians, therefore, would do anything possible to neutralize the new system by increasing their offensive capability.

What does "Star Wars" actually propose to do? Using a vast network of hundreds or perhaps thousands of machines in space, in the air, and on the ground — all of which must work together with absolute precision — it seeks to intercept and destroy every possible incoming enemy warhead. And while the ABM systems of the 1960's dealt only with the "terminal" phase of a missile's flight, SDI calls for additional layers of defense directed at the earlier phases of an attack. Missiles that escaped one layer would be subsequently attacked by the next.

During the "blast" phase of an enemy launch, the missile must be located and tracked by satellite sensors, and its flight path relayed to a weapons platform in space. The space-based laser beam must then be perfectly aimed over thousands of miles, and locked to its target long enough to burn out the missile's warhead fuse circuitry.

Aiming these laser beams, which travel at the approximate speed of light, requires massive and complex systems of space-based relay mirrors. If this ballistic missile defense (BMD) system is to provide total protection, there is no room for *any* margin of error.

Incoming missiles which escaped destruction during the boost phase would then have to be intercepted during the "busing" phase, after the rocket engines had burned out. At this point, the ICBM's nose cone disgorges a "bus" carrying a number of multiple independently targeted reentry vehicles (MIRV's), which are released one by one toward their separate targets. The BDM system would here have to discriminate between 10 real warheads and 100 decoys in order to save the time and fuel that would be wasted on tracking harmless junk.

If, during a major attack, even 10% of the reentry vehicles (RV's) got through, a "threat cloud" of 1,000 bombs and 10,000 decoys would require the last-minute interception of 12 targets per second by space lasers, ground lasers, and ABM's if total protection were to be guaranteed.[9]

The difficulties outlined so far do not take into account the relatively simple measures the Soviets might employ to challenge this extraordinary plan. First, they could fit their ICBM's with more powerful engines, reducing the available time for interception during the boost phase. Second, they could coat their missiles with heat-resistant material which would greatly increase the time and energy needed by the lasers to burn out the circuitry. Third, they could release a whole host of electronic gadgets to jam and confound the U.S. tracking signals. Finally, even the most perfect BDM system would never be able to track a weapon already in existence — the small, pilotless, ground-hugging inscrutable Cruise Missile, which does not travel in space and therefore cannot be stopped by air defense systems.

It is clear to everyone that computers must play a critical role in the systems that SDI is considering. Accordingly, the Strategic Defense Initiative Organization (SDIO) convened a Panel on Computing in Support of Battle Management. This Panel was asked to identify the computer science problems that would have to be solved in order to guarantee an effective BMD system. David Lorge Parnas, a member of the Panel, submitted to SDIO in July 1985, together with his resignation, a technical report containing eight papers which explain in ordinary English why this system cannot be built.[10] In the conclusion of the introductory paper, "Why the SDI Software System Will be Untrustworthy", he states: "All of the cost estimates indicate that this will be the most massive software project ever attempted. The system has numerous technical characteristics that will make it more difficult than previous systems, independent of size. Because of the extreme demands on the system and our inability to test it, we will never be able to believe, with any confidence, that we have succeeded. Nuclear weapons will remain a threat."

Further, in a paper entitled "Can Program Verification Make the SDI Software Reliable?", he concludes: "It is inconceivable to me that one could provide a convincing proof of correctness of even a small portion of SDI software. Given our inability to specify our requirements[11] of the software, I do not know what such a proof would mean if I had it."

And finally, in "Is SDI an Efficient Way to Fund Worthwhile

Research?", he replies: "There is no justification for continuing with the pretense that the SDI battle management software can be built just to obtain funding for otherwise worthwhile programs. DoD's (Department of Defense's) approach to research management requires a thorough evaluation and review."

The notion of introducing destructive weapons into space does not appear to have any advantages at all; on the contrary, it would divert billions of dollars away from essential human requirements as yet unmet on Earth. If people in the West are concerned about this unfortunate turn of events, they should urge the U.S. Government to cancel this program, and in its place to reaffirm and strengthen the ABM Treaty of 1972, thereby signalling to the Soviets a saner view of where our best interests lie.

In crisis relocation and "Star Wars" we have examined two rather pathetic schemes to ward off the insurmountable. The facts speak plainly for themselves. Neither approach has any real prospect of success, and indeed both are dangerous and misleading because they minimize appreciation of the danger by fantasizing the illusion of survival. Survival as we understand it, by any humane or civilized standard of life on this planet, would not be possible after a nuclear war. The prospect of defense against it, therefore, can and will only exist in the minds of those too deluded or lacking in courage to confront the actual facts.

Any civil defense planning in the nuclear age further suggests that nuclear war is an acceptable eventuality, one to be prepared for and overcome, such as an earthquake or a flood. But earthquakes and floods, and the bombs of World War II, are of a different order of magnitude than are exploding nuclear suns. Nuclear fission-fusion bombs present an unparalleled threat to mankind, and therefore require an unparalleled response. This response is not to be found in the physical dimension, in the military-industrial world of concrete and lasers. It lies, rather, in the dimension and depth of the human spirit, in the unifying bonds of communication and friendship.

Part III

Preparing to Act

CHAPTER 7

THE NIGHTMARE:
Inside the Mind of the Strategist

The purpose of this part of the book is to prepare the average citizen with a clear and simple understanding of the fundamentals of the arms race, so that he may substitute a confidence in his grasp of the matter for the feeling that only the "experts" can deal with it.

Most of us think of nuclear strategy as a complex and secret affair, one quite beyond our ability to comprehend. This modest, compliant attitude is very convenient for the experts, who are left free to play out their nuclear fantasies, or computer "scenarios", at what the population believes to be a skilled and professional level.

We shall see, however, in the next few pages of plain English, that the great military strategies of our day boil down to a few fairly simple concepts — concepts which can be readily understood by the citizens of a democracy, and which may therefore be trusted to their inspection and judgement. And it should go without saying that any normal person whose life is threatened by these intrigues has a natural right to information about them, and the corresponding authority to evaluate them.

To begin with, then, all nuclear strategy proceeds from the basic assumption that nuclear weapons, having been invented, cannot be disinvented, and are therefore here to stay. Not only here to stay, but to haunt us with uneasiness and put the world on tenterhooks whenever conflict flares. Without them, the story goes, the West would be defenseless against nuclear attack, and would be opening the door to nuclear blackmail. Furthermore, it is argued, as the ultimate source of terror they are the one and only means of balancing world power. So in terms of this dreadful but unavoidable, this unfortunate but inevitable fact of life, they have become the cornerstone of Western military policy.

We shall refer to this belief in nuclear weapons as the absolute and indispensable custodian of world security as "nuclearism". Nuclearism — this strange hold that the weapons have on the human mind — actually resembles a cult or a superstition, because the weapons are at once both magic and curse. Curse, because we cannot disinvent them and apparently cannot control our thoughts about them; and magic because they are seen as preserving the miracle of peace.

They are a visitation, a plague, it seems, that breed themselves uncontrollably and consume us, wrecking world economies and terrorizing children in their wake. But, according to the experts (or the "nuclear priesthood") we simply must face up to their preordained existence in a mature, adult way. We have to be stoical. There is no other option.

What makes nuclearism a superstition is that man has lodged a power in these inanimate weapons that has caused him to abandon his own reason. Not only do the weapons fail utterly to achieve peace and stability, but they hold the whole of human civilization, past, present, and future — and everything else's past, present, and future, for that matter — at the point of instant and total annihilation.

This chapter contends that the moment one accepts this belief in the inevitability of nuclear weapons, a dense thicket of political and military contradictions springs up in one's path. The thicket is so dark and overgrown that no light can enter it, nor any wit untangle it.

The inevitability assumption is like a crumbling cornerstone laid as the foundation for the entire discussion, yet nothing can be built upon it, and every conclusion proceeding from it is riddled with contradictions. And it is because the inevitability assumption is so widely accepted that the public can get nowhere thinking about it and therefore lacks confidence in addressing the issue. As we shall see, the experts get no further themselves.

*　　*　　*

From the time the Soviets exploded their first atomic bomb in August, 1949, the arms race was on, and nuclear deployment strategy was born. During the decades that followed, American strategic policy developed several varied and confusing faces, for it needed to succeed simultaneously at a number of levels: 1) the level of maintaining public support, by reassuring the American taxpayer that a very frightening game, though expensive to play, was safe and under control; 2) the level of using early American superiority to bluff the Soviets into submission where conflicts over "vital interests" occurred; and 3) the level of actual intentions and deployments, which are classified, secret activities, and therefore not accountable to the American people.

We shall begin with the first — the official, vote-getting, tax-supported public policy. It is, simply, that though the United States must have nuclear weapons as security against possible enemy aggression, their actual use must be avoided at all costs.

A policy of never using the weapons has dictated that they be strategically deployed in such a way that neither side will ever be tempted to use them *first*. The logic emerged that if the Soviet Union, in hoping to gain an advantage by firing nuclear missiles at the United States, knew *for sure* that there would result a prompt and massive retaliation upon itself, then the Soviet Union would never carry out such an attack. This is the principle of *deterrence,* in which the aggressor is punished as much as the victim.

As nuclear principles go, deterrence is rather an optimistic one, because it restricts its interest to the period in a conflict leading up to, but not actually including, the outbreak of nuclear war. Deterrence plans preventively, optimistically, for non-war. So within the cult of nuclearism (that is, within the assumption that we must have the weapons at all), deterrence may be seen to proceed from a relatively sane and hopeful frame of mind — at least if such words can be applied to anything nuclear.

If the principle of deterrence is to work in practice, neither side must ever be in a position to strike quickly and knock out the retaliatory defenses of the other side. In other words, neither side can be allowed to develop the confidence that it could destroy its enemy's nuclear arsenal in a surprise attack. To keep this confidence from developing, two essential conditions must be maintained: 1) that civilian populations on both sides be vulnerable to attack, which is the *price* of aggression, in that either aggressor may expect to lose his population through retaliation; and 2) that weapons on both sides be largely invulnerable to attack, which is the *guarantee of retaliation* to an aggressor. The first condition is often described as mutual assured destruction (MAD), and involves the targeting of large population centers on both sides, a kind of reciprocal blackmail against attack. The second condition involves a variety of measures which either conceal or protect a nation's nuclear arsenal from the enemy. For example, the United States achieves invulnerability in its submarine fleet through underwater concealment; it protects its long-range bombers by keeping some airborne at all times; and it houses its land-based intercontinental ballistic missiles (ICBM's) in hardened silos. These three forces, each representing an arm of the military system, are together known as the TRI-AD, and each one has more than enough weapons to destroy the entire Soviet population. It is inconceivable — particularly considering the untrackable nuclear submarine fleet — that even the best-timed, most coordinated Soviet surprise attack could destroy enough American warheads to prevent a thoroughly devastating American retaliation. And the same is true vice-versa.

For as long as military reliance on nuclear weapons exists, deterrence must be the overriding principle, at least if our goal is to avoid war. Deterrence has worked since the 1950's, and what it deters is nuclear war. It owes its success partly to the universal dread of nuclear war, and partly to the mercy of the heavens that there has not been an accident.

Though the bread of American nuclearism has always been buttered by public confidence in deterrence, behind the scenes things have been much less straightforward. As the nuclear age has unfolded, certain pressures have been swaying U.S. policy away from the caution of deterrence and towards a preparedness to fight a "limited nuclear war". The first pressure to emerge was the very early Soviet rejection of deterrence. Russia, having been ravaged by countless invasions over hundreds of years, and having lost 20 million lives in World War II, has a chronic, obsessive concern with the security of her borders. Consequently, the Soviet analysts have been unwilling to base their defense on a policy (deterrence) which credits the enemy with the good sense to refrain from attacking.

It is difficult for the Western mind to grasp the impact of this memory of loss and violation upon the Soviet people. The United States, on the other hand, historically free of border paranoia, is psychologically equipped to trust the optimism of deterrence.

As a result of this profound insecurity, Soviet attention has focused on the more sinister side of the nuclear game — the tactics of actually fighting and winning a nuclear war, "if it is unleashed by the imperialists".[1] They believe that any nuclear exchange would almost certainly lead to all-out war, and when the damage was finally tallied, the most prepared side would have "won".[2]

Accordingly, the Soviets have been competing to develop actual war-fighting advantages, such as greater numbers of weapons, the ability to strike enemy arsenals quickly and effectively should war begin, and a widespread civil defense program to enhance population survival. It is not surprising that this apparent

Soviet willingness to go the whole way has shaken U.S. confidence in deterrence, a principle which to work must be trusted by both sides.

A second problem with deterrence is the contradiction that while deterrence implies a defensive posture on both sides, the superpowers do not behave very defensively at all; they are engaged, rather, in an active, competitive struggle for world supremacy. That this struggle may originate in mutual fear does not make it any the less aggressive in outcome. It was in direct contradiction to the principle of deterrence, for example, that the United States, which enjoyed nuclear superiority for the first twenty years, yielded to the temptation to use nuclear threats in "defense" of its interests abroad. This was evidenced in Korea (1953), Indochina (1954), Lebanon (1958), Laos (1961), Berlin (1961), Cuba (1962), and Viet Nam (1969-72).[3] These threats stopped when the Soviets caught up in the early nineteen-seventies. (The Soviets have not been reported as making such threats.)

This American use of nuclear diplomacy to protect "vital interests" abroad has backfired somewhat. For example, when the United States withdrew from Viet Nam *without* following through on its threats, it destroyed the credibility that it would ever in fact do so. This behavior demonstrates the absurdity of placing confidence in a weapon that cannot realistically be used. Through this mutually misplaced confidence, both countries are reduced to a fundamentally weak position. The weakness, in turn, explains the ridiculous postures that each has assumed in its struggles to out-manoeuvre the other.

The United States, on the one hand, demonstrates its "resolve" by threatening a limited first strike on a Soviet military target. This "involves a lethal war of nerves, a reckless raising of the ante in a winner-take-all game of geopolitical poker. The central objective is to convince the Soviet leadership that we believe in this limited war scenario enough to embark on it. If they believe in our recklessness, it is always prudent for them to back down."[4]

On the other hand, the "Soviet swagger" guarantees the escalation of any limited strike to an all-out nuclear holocaust, and to prove *its* "resolve", the USSR spends billions on post-war survival shelters.

In sharp contrast to these posturings, the fact remains that it is deterrence and only deterrence which ultimately dictates the behavior of each side, *whatever* they may say. In the words of Leon Wieseltier, "The strategy is determined by the weapon. The missiles have only to exist, and deterrence is the law of their existence. For this reason the Soviet Union acts in accordance with the doctrine of deterrence even if it does not think in accordance with it."[5] So hand in hand with the threats and the bluffs, we now see both sides modernizing and enlarging their conventional naval forces in an effort to bring usable and believable military strength to scenes of world conflict.

It is at least becoming clear that we are running out of ways to mask absolute weakness (the inability to resort to force at all as a method of conflict resolution in the nuclear age) with the appearance of strength (the "recklessness" and the "swaggering"). It should have been clear from the outset that force and threats of force could no longer be used as the basis for settling disputes. Yet this extravaganza of nuclearism presses on, mocking millions of diseased and hungry people, and dogging man's peace of mind worldwide.

Having looked at certain political aspects of nuclear strategy, both foreign and domestic, we will now turn briefly to military theory itself.

*   *   *

It has been said that *in the abstract,* "war is an act of force, and there is no logical limit to the application of that force. Each side therefore, compels its opponent to follow suit; a reciprocal action is started which must lead, in theory, to extremes . . . a clash of forces operating and obedient to no law but their own." Absolute war, however, is "nothing but a play of the imagination . . . If we were to think purely in absolute terms, we could avoid every difficulty by a stroke of the pen and proclaim with inflexible logic that, since the extreme must always be the goal, the greatest effort must always be exerted."[6]

The foregoing classical analysis describes the essence of the arms race, which is that there is no theoretical limit to it. And yet the thoughts which spring from the unlimited imaginations of military strategists are actually being played out at staggering expense in the real world.

The thinking runs roughly as follows. First, they ask, what if deterrence fails and war begins? Once a war has begun, our foremost objective must be to limit damage to our side by knocking out Soviet missiles before they are launched. (The use of antiballistic missile interceptors — ABM's — was, incidentally, almost totally banned by the SALT I treaty of 1972.) But here the problem arises that if one side were to achieve this capability for damage limitation, it would, by the same token, be in a position to launch a successful first strike against the other side. The other side would then begin to fear a first strike, and would reason that because it was vulnerable to surprise attack, perhaps it should take the initiative itself (or "pre-empt") by attacking first. So there is a difficult trade-off between achieving damage limitation, on the one hand, and minimizing the enemy's incentive towards launching a preventive first strike on the other.

It is in the best interests of both sides to take into account, when deploying new weapons, how nervous they are apt to make the other side feel, and to keep one another's anxieties at bay. Accordingly, a second goal of nuclear strategy is "crisis stability", which is the state of balance required to keep the fears of both sides under control during a brink-of-war crisis, and thereby reduce the risk of one side panicking with a pre-emptive first strike.

If crisis stability were the only concern of American planners, they would build such an invulnerable arsenal of missiles that the Soviets could never believe a Soviet first strike would succeed. At the same time, they would act to ease Soviet fears of an American first strike by building inaccurate missiles with long flight times. These combined American actions would minimize the fears of first strike on both sides, by making each secure in the knowledge that the other could not be profitably tempted to try one.

But here another trade-off arises. Slow, inaccurate American weapons would reduce the credibility, to the Soviets, of an effective U.S. retaliation, should the Soviets begin a war. This puts crisis stability, a hair-trigger matter of overwhelming importance, at odds with the basic principle of deterrence.

A further objective of both sides is to control the escalation of the bombing, once war has begun. From the American standpoint, the principle of escalation control is to deny the Soviets any advantages that might be gained by escalating the bombing. This principle is subdivided into "escalation matching", in which nuclear forces are designed to fight a war at whatever level the enemy chooses; and "escalation dominance", which attempts to gain superiority at every level of combat the enemy chooses, and to thereby shift the burden of escalation to him. But once again, the degree to which escalation dominance is achieved is the degree to which enemy fears of first strike are increased, so that escalation dominance succeeds at the expense of crisis stability. *The inescapable paradox of nuclearism is that both sides wish to gain superiority without frightening the other side.* Trapped in this paradox like two rats in a maze, each adversary must think for the other, so that as a team they may secure their *mutual* goal, the prevention of nuclear war. In the final analysis they are *working together* against the presumed necessary existence of the weapons! It is the blackest irony of all time, this superstitious cult of nuclearism.

The Nightmare

Another critical objective in nuclear war fighting is the ability to negotiate an end to war, and quickly. But there is a contradiction between damage limitation, which seeks to "decapitate" the enemy leadership by early destruction of command and control headquarters, and war termination, which requires the survival of a leader to negotiate with.

A final goal of nuclear strategy is to reduce nuclear costs and risks through arms control. Arms control is basically unattractive to strategists because it interferes with their intricate plans to balance all of the foregoing (and fundamentally irreconcilable) objectives. It is also difficult because new weapons technology outpaces the poorly funded arms control efforts to identify, limit, and count (or verify) one another's weapons.

In summary, we see that strategic goals can be divided into two groups: those which emphasize war avoidance, and those which presuppose war fighting. These two sets of goals (see Table 2) are at absolute loggerheads: to the extent that one set succeeds, the other set fails.

War Avoidance	War Fighting
Deterrence	Damage Limitation
Crisis Stability	Escalation Control
Arms Control	War Termination
	Arms Increase

Table 2

What emerges is a fundamental conflict between the demands of peace and the demands of war. This is the essential folly of the underlying inevitability assumption of nuclearism.

*   *   *

What could be worse, one might ask, then indulging all these billions of tax dollars in this insatiable, self-defeating, contradiction-ridden cult of nuclearism? What *is* worse is that armaments technology is advancing so quickly, in terms of the speed and accuracy of weapons delivery, that the time available during a crisis for leaders to consider the foregoing complexities has all but disappeared. If and when the fated hour comes for the decision of ultimate survival, decades of scenario development on both sides will be compressed into a moment which will permit little more consideration than the flip of a coin. In all likelihood, impulse will prevail.

To illustrate this, the newly recognized phenomenon of the electromagnetic pulse (EMP) has in recent years created the awesome feasibility of a successful first strike. Let us suppose, for example, that in a carefully coordinated first strike offensive the Soviets were to launch several hundred ICBM's at the United States, with the intention of knocking out the same number of American ICBM's. Until the EMP was factored into the calculations, the 25-30 minute flight-time of the Soviet missiles would have easily allowed the United States to release a large volley of its own ICBM's in return. But if in conjunction with the attack the Soviets were to fire four or five submarine launched ballistic missiles (SLBM's) from patrols off America's Atlantic coast, things would be very different. Within seven minutes of launching, these SLBM's could be exploded at various points some 300 miles above continental America, producing instant nationwide electrical and communications blackouts from the electromagnetic pulse.

In the meantime, it would have taken two minutes for the first U.S. satellite detection of an attack in progress to reach the American command. This would allow a scant five minutes for the U.S. command to make and transmit to its bases the ultimate decision for nuclear war. The bases, in turn, would have only minutes or seconds to act before their launchers were "pinned down" by the short-circuiting effect of the electro-magnetic pulse.

This shorting effect of the EMP is regarded by analysts as the most critical problem of all. The strategic response to its harrowing time frame is to "launch under attack", or more popularly, to "use 'em or lose 'em".

We are thus approaching the end of deterrence: in a desperate move to preserve it, we declare to the Soviets that a mere launch warning will result in instant and total nuclear war, and they reply that any war will be all-out.

Though large defense sums have been committed to installing anti-EMP equipment within appropriate electrical systems, there is no guarantee that a return to the more comfortable 25-30 minute decision period will be possible. Meanwhile, the 5-minute dilemma is a constant pressure on both sides to settle the issue conclusively and advantageously by surprise attack. It is rather like the man who was promised a million dollars if he could walk across a bridge without thinking about a white elephant. The temptation to resolve the nuclear paradox once and for all, get the suspension over with, must be as persistent as the unwanted elephant. In one case the man is paid not to think about an elephant; in the other he is told not to use weapons which are built for use and are ever-presently in mind. Both positions are logically ridiculous and intolerable to endure.

To put it another way, does the finger pull the trigger, or does the trigger pull the finger?

So here we are in the 1980's, trusting in a deterrence antiquated by technology and all but in shambles. The two adversaries now stand nose to nose in the forest clearing, each sizzling with hand grenades, waiting for the other to twitch. Is it not time to something *different* about the problem?

To conclude our observations on the cult of nuclearism, its proponents are laying out, in the real world of children, birds, trees, blue sky, and sunlight, the game of absolute war, of the "greatest effort" that Clausewitz described as possible only in the imagination. The nuclear mind has lost touch with sanity and reality.

We shall now step outside the military maze and look down upon it from above, to see its participants as mental prisoners trapped in a nightmare game which will dissolve like a dream if they can only wake up.

CHAPTER 8

THE GAME:
Beyond the Mind of the Nuclear Strategist

Perhaps the most striking feature of human intelligence is its ability to examine problems from different points of view. If one frame of reference or point of view fails to yield a solution, we try another, and another, until sooner or later we arrive at a perspective which permits a view of the solution.

Most of us have experienced this unexpectedly at one time or another. Say, for sample, we have spent half an hour struggling with a tricky problem, and in exasperation we step back from it. Suddenly, through that change in focus, we "see" it. It is like refocusing a lens to produce a different view of the information. The answer can seem painfully obvious in retrospect.

We experience this change in perspective as a moment of insight or enlightenment — as the instant when everything falls into place. Such insights usually relate to technical problems, which run the gamut from rearranging furniture to designing a space shuttle. But the moment of insight is always the same: a person steps out of being "stuck" in an unproductive point of view, and in that expanded moment lies the answer.

It is with much greater difficulty, however, that people step outside their usual points of view in handling problems with other people. It means studying *oneself* in the context of the problem with as much detachment as one might assess a broken window. This means creating a *division* in the self, a division between the habitual self, which is immersed in its needs, satisfactions, and disappointments; and the objective, analytical self, which separates off and stands back to observe the behavior of the immersed self.

This is more easily said than done. The difficulty lies in the totality of the immersed self, which when in charge tends to fill the vessel of consciousness in an absolute and indivisible way. The trick is to keep the observer on call, so to speak, in a small but accessible corner of the mind, and to be ready to shift gears when necessary.

Children are born into simple, emotional natures, and many remain there for life, never learning to identify a perspective which would allow them to understand the problems they encounter with other people. As Carl Jung, the Swiss psychologist, so elegantly phrased it:

> "The psychological rule says that when an inner situation is not made conscious, it happens outside, as fate. That is to say, when the individual remains undivided and does not become conscious of his inner contradictions, the world must perforce act out the conflict and be torn into opposite halves."[1]

This is worth remembering, for conflicts which tear the external world apart may alternatively be solved from within.

In the last chapter we looked at military strategy from its own point of view, and there found irreconcilable difficulties. Now we shall back up and away from that point of view, and focus in on it from afar, as if through a large telescope.

Imagine that you are slowly approaching our globe as a guest in a spaceship manned by foreign scholars of the Planet Earth. Through your telescope you see men in offices in Washington and Moscow, poring over desks, chin-in-hand in deep concentration. You comment aloud that if these opponents were sitting over the same table they might well be playing chess. You are informed that the adversaries are in fact adhering to prearranged game-like rules. Years ago, for example, they agreed to limit themselves to offensive weapons only. The competition would be infinitely consuming, they realized, if its terms were to include both ICBM's and antiballistic missiles. If each ICBM or SLBM were to be neutralized by an awaiting ABM, both sides would have to build more ICBM's to ensure that some would get through. In turn, each side would need more ABM's to guarantee itself a defense. The futility of such an offensive-defensive arms race thus led them to virtually ban ABM's in the ABM Treaty of 1972.

There were also the vast and disconcerting possibilities of basing missiles in outer space and upon the ocean floors. So to avoid a free-for-all that would consume every dollar and ruble that was printed, they limited the battleground to a kind of chessboard, by the Outer Space Treaty of 1967 and the Seabed Arms Control Treaty of 1971.

This contest had all the features of a game: the "board" was geographically limited; the "pieces" (delivery vehicles) were limited to bombers, ships, and ICBM's; and the "moves" were limited to the offensive.

As your spaceship approaches Earth, you feel bewilderment beginning to grow. What is happening on Earth is not really a war, you reflect, because there is no actual fighting. It is not really a game, either, because the contestants are so grim. And the term "cold war" does not explain its mutually agreed terms, for all is fair in love and war — cold or otherwise. Then it occurs to you that it resembles a duel, where men fight it out with deadly weapons according to prearranged rules. But the weapons are so deadly in this case that both sides would be killed. Does this war-game-duel just go on and on until one side drops from *economic* exhaustion? But exhaustion produces despair, and despair urges first strike. If one side begins to win, you realize, the whole world stands to lose. Is there no way out for these Earthlings?

Then comes a flash of insight: if these "warriors" can agree upon the rules of their game, they are only a step away from calling it off altogether! After all, the rules themselves presuppose a

89

measure of trust and cooperation. Or do these contestants *prefer* to live in suspicion and fear, under the dark threat of annihilation?

The answer is that *they cannot escape from their points of view*. They are "stuck" in their dilemma, and in the belief thta they must endure it.

The ability to escape from one's point of view begins with a special realization. And it begins *only* if one sees that in saying "I", one does not refer to a single or constant thing. Looking at the body, of course, it appears that "I" is a single and constant thing, but often "I" does not refer to the body at all.

"I" is felt to refer to one's center of conscious awareness, as though it were an indivisable, homogeneous, and deliberating point of being. In fact, however, consciousness is made up of a tumbling diversity of fleeting and contradictory sensations, thoughts, and feelings: "I" would like to lose weight, but "I" cannot resist this cheesecake (pride vs. appetite); "I" love my husband but "I" desire John Henry (compassion vs. arousal); "I" feel like a coward because "I'm" afraid of heights (guilt vs. vertigo); "I" was raised as an Anglican but "I" have become a Taoist (circumstance vs. choice); "I" love the sun but "I" get easily burned (warmth vs. pain); "I" cannot decide whether to watch the golf or the tennis (deliberation); "I" must remember to phone Aunt Matilda (conscience); "I" feel sleepy (drowsiness); "I" had an adventure dream last night (subconscious); "I" adore floppy hats! (fun); "I" could kill whoever slashed my tires (anger); "I" love Bach (joy); "I" feel blue (mood); "I'm" going to throw a party (impulse).

The majority of these "I"'s refer to the host of thoughts, memories, desires, impulses, trainings, hungers, sensations, and moods that make up human consciousness. These "I"'s are in no way consistent with one another. Nor are they invited into consciousness or deliberately experienced by the individual — they simply happen to us; they well up from within our depths, one after another, in a steady, unforeen flow. We shall henceforth refer to these unsolicited conscious events as "little i" experiences, and to the overall stream of such experiences as the "automatic self".

These "little i" experiences are not only common to all conscious creatures, but they have guided their evolution — though in the animal kingdom they have not been internally verbalized. The vast majority of these "i"'s simply reflect a creature's (whether man or animal) heredity and environment. They reveal man largely as a product of pre-existing forces: "i" am black; "i" love baseball; "i" hate spinach; "i" am a Democrat; "i" speak French.

These culturally determined conditions, beliefs, values, opinions, likes, and dislikes combine to produce in consciousness a fairly predictable assortment of little "i"'s. This inner conglomerate translates into an equally consistent outward appearance, manifest through dress, posture, movement, and facial set. The trained eye thus recognizes at a glance the cultural traits of a Greek, German, American, Englishman, or Swede — though all are white Caucasians.

So the sum of all these little "i"'s represents the total way in which an individual's culture and make-up have acted upon him. This is not to deny the incredible complexity of the human being, or his capacity for free will. It is simply to say that when he is experientially immersed within one of his little "i"'s, he is functioning essentially as a machine, as he has done, along with the animals, since time began.

If a man lives through his entire life without standing back to examine his own collection of little "i"'s, he remains purely and simply a product of his past, just as an animal does. He remains fully immersed in and obedient to the collection of little "i"'s which taken together we have already described as the automatic or conditioned or programmed self. This level of the self has, by definition, no more capacity to change its ingrained, cultural points of view than has a cat to swear off mice.

So the man of unexamined self is like a vessel which is already full — full of its own culture and its own past. In fact he *is* the culture, the living personification of the culture. And as might be expected, when he meets an individual from a different kind of culture — a person who is fully stuck in *his* point of view — then they cannot have room for one another; they cannot be receptive to one another because they are already full. And when contentious issues arise they cannot listen to one another, and are therefore reduced to the use of force. This is our history and heritage as human beings.

Now here is the rub. When a person recognizes that a large part of his being is operating at a purely predictable, mechanical level, what part of him is doing that recognizing? It is another part altogether. It is a part of the self which is *not* automatic, and which may stand apart and observe the train of experiences which flow into consciousness. In the process of this observation, it may choose *not* to act, believe, or even feel, in the ways that are presented by the automatic self.

This ability to separate the watchful observer from the automatic self is the uniquely human phenomenon that allows man to choose his destiny. It separates man from the animals, who are bonded to their natures, who indeed *are* their natures. It is what Krishnamurti has called "the observer", what Jung referred to as the "divided" self, and what Ouspensky distinguished as "magnetic center", or as "real" or "permanent" I. We shall refer to it as "Big I". It is what we will have used if we ever find the solution to war. And to use it, we will need to place an overriding priority on developing it — in our homes, schools, churches, friendships, work sites, media — everywhere.

When a person comes to the realization that his beliefs, attitudes, values, and opinions have been circumstantially shaped by the time and place of his birth — when he recognizes this *fact*, he has begun to see himself as a single being relative to the whole of life. He is no longer absolutely what "little i" is. He is not a "right" or a "wrong" human being; not a "better" or

The Game

a "worse" human being; he is simply *another* human being.

It would not occur to such a person to fight with another person simply because that person's society was differently organized than his own. On the contrary, he would fight only if attacked, or perhaps very hungry, or if his family were threatened, or the like. But many Western countries (and Russia, too) are being maintained, at crucifying expense, in a state of "readiness" for war. This current readiness depends upon the maintenance of a war psychology in these large tax-paying populations. To maintain a war psychology means fostering the individual's sense that he is being continually threatened in a basic way. This depends upon leadership's ability to stimulate the unexamined beliefs, values, and opinions of the collective "little i" self, and to persuade "little i" everywhere that "the enemy" is cruel, aggressive, and treacherous.

When this attempted persuasion succeeds with the majority of people in two nations at one time, then the conditions for war exist. Sometimes they exist with legitimate cause, proceeding from a real threat, as when Hitler overran Europe; and other times they proceed from a merely *possible* threat. To the extent that people are trapped in their "little i" points of view is the extent to which they risk turning the possibility of war into the probability of war.

This is not an obvious point. The crux of it is, that until "little i" is recognized and brought under control, it will project its own dark side — its primitive capacities for aggression, mistrust, and deceit — into the mind of the enemy *whether they are already there or not*. So in this most fundamental way, war begins in the imagination, and gains credibility through failure to observe the automatic self.

It is only when man sees and quiets these "little i" thoughts, when he empties his mind to make it fresh and receptive, that he may become able to truly observe the "enemy", as he actually is, *in fact*[2] — and no longer in the light of expectation.

It hardly needs saying that East-West relations have proceeded from the smallest of "i"'s. By the same token, the opportunities for improvement are great. How might Western diplomacy invite such improvement, and from whence might the energy come?

The separation of "Big I" from "little i" is a learned ability, one that strengthens and grows with time. People who have learned it often take it for granted and find it difficult to credit that others have not. They do not recongize that its absence stems from ignorance of this evolving potential of the human mind. And ignorance, by definition, is not deliberate; it is deprivation of knowledge and understanding. So men are driven to power and violence not by a preference for negative emotion, but by the dull and limited mind which has not learned to distinguish the forces which act upon "little i". And if the formative influences have been harsh or distorted, it is all the more crucial for a person to balance his perspective by learning to summon "Big I".

Given the entrenched "little i" thinking of conservative militarism, and the widespread economic gains accruing from the arms race, from where will new perspectives emerge?

Until recently it has seemed unlikely that new visions of human interaction would be coming out of the Soviet Union, though it is now looking more possible. The Soviets, with their frozen landscapes and war-torn history, are a grim and stoical people not much given to optimism. The Soviet reality is that the use and acceptance of state force to control the domestic population betrays a limited commitment to the social values of trust and cooperation. It would take time, therefore, perhaps generations, for the Soviets to evolve a more inspired vision of what life could be. At bottom, the issue revolves around confidence, or faith. What the imagination has the faith to project is what shapes the things to come.

So if the process is to occur at all, it seems more likely that it will begin in the West, where government resistance to the will of the people is less open and brutal. In the West the people have at least the constitutional machinery to allow them to be truly self-governing, should they decide to use it.

But the West has its own problems. It seems that almost by definition the controlling political and economic forces have been compelled towards power by the fearing imagination of "little i". These ruling forces are frequently unreflective, paranoid, and short-term in outlook, and together their energies add up to the chilling momentum described below:

> "We go on piling weapon upon weapon, missile upon missile, new levels of destructiveness upon old ones . . . helplessly, almost involuntarily: like the victims of some sort of hypnosis, like men in a dream, like lemmings headed for the sea, like the children of Hamelin marching blindly behind their Pied Piper."[3]

The military-industrial complex is a formidable force in the Western world, and is steadily accelerated by advancing technology. It includes not only military personnel, but the arms, missiles, and tank contractors; the communications, electronics, and computer industries; the aeronautics and shipbuilding industries, and countless other support services. In 1983, military expenditures consumed some 6.6% of the U.S. Gross National Product, and some 26.8% of its federal budget.[4]

All those who earn their livelihood through these activities are a force of inertia against disarmament. And though we see the phenomenon of retired top-level military personnel speaking out against the arms race (see Appendix I), we would not expect leadership from those still employed.

Nor is effective leadership likely to emerge from the academic pursuits of science and technology. Our knowledge of the world has become so detailed and intricate that a displacement factor has settled in. For minds committed to science and technology there is little time left over for other reflections. And "Big I" international relations problem-solving takes not only time and maturity, but a shift in emphasis from the outer (technological) to the inner (emotional) landscape. It requires a fundamental appreciation of the difference in quality between knowledge and wisdom. And though there have been some outstanding humanists within the scientific community, the mind-set itself tends to seek technical rather than psychological solutions. Intelligence and knowledge will not by themselves lead us out of the arms quandary, and the expectation that "they" — the intelligentsia in the universities, laboratories, and research institutes — will somehow protect us is sadly misplaced.

What if the United States were to elect a president who was absolutely determined to demilitarize American international relations? We hear about the "extensive" powers of the U.S. president, but if he is out of sync with the system he can be curtailed in many ways.

As senior bureaucrats know, there is usually a power struggle between the elected government with its limited term of office and its slate of political objectives on the one hand, and the ongoing bureaucracy, with its needs for comfort and stability on the other. Should a president threaten the U.S. military bureaucracy in this way, it would do everything in the book to deter him. It would overwhelm him with statistics on Soviet arms and expenditures; it would produce documents regarding Soviet expansionist intentions; it would drag its feet with plausible concerns at every point along the way. It short, it would simply out-wait his term of office.

Military bureaucracies, like all others, are driven like biological organisms to survive and grow. To demilitarize the U.S.-Soviet conflict, therefore, a determined president would need widespread establishment support to convert the resources of the military-industrial complex into comprehensvie international programs that would meet pressing human needs.[5] But the establishment is too comfortable to voluntarily transform itself.

The Game

Nothing will change until a mass groundswell of public pressure is directed against the power, prestige, and profits of the permanent war economy. But first the public must wake up to the reality that *only* a mass human effort can halt the tragic momentum that is now underway.

The people who are attracted to this military network view human relationships as implicitly founded upon conflict and aggression. This implicit assumption blocks their vision of man's capacity for imagining a better world, and of his qualities of optimism, faith, and determination to build one. Lacking this vision, they project into their weapons the primitive animal violence which has settled disputes since the dawn of time. And from the certainty of their cynicism they take heroic pride in their technological might.

The resulting irony is a weapon of cosmic destructive force in the hands of men whose aggressiveness has been outmoded by the very weapon they wield.

Why does this strange paradox persist? Again, it is because man does not see that he has choice; he is blinded to his options by his traditional point of view.

It is like Plato's analogy of the cave, where men were born and lived in underground caves lit only by fire. In the flickering light haunted by shadows they believed this subterranean twilight was all there was. One day they discovered the great world above, and their demons dissolved in the light of the sun.

Man is now confronted with a choice for survival. The choice lies in the duality of his own psyche. It is the choice between the reactive animal and the self-reflective human being. It is the choice between righteousness and compassion, between point of view and overview, between nation and world, and ultimately between extinction and survival.

But the choice cannot be left to the philosophic few. It must take the form of an evolutionary leap, a pervasive transformation in the unit of mankind.[6]

In the meantime the weapons stand poised on the horizon in bleak testimony to the prevailing forces of cynicism and despair. These forces may only prevail, however, as long as *each person* succumbs to them. The solution, like the problem, is in the mind of the individual. But there is still time: the world is yet intact, and opportunity awaits.

CHAPTER 9

THE CLASSIC FORCES FOR CHANGE:
Power, Imagination, and Love

In this section we have been looking at what we have *got* in a far from reassuring world. What we have got (a plant in jitters, poised for destruction) has been brought into existence by preoccupation with the things we do *not want*: weakness, exploitation, war, and death. We have been trapped in the mind-set of trying to avoid the undesirable.

It is *not possible* to nurture what we *do* want from the seeds of fear. Try it. Try to invite useful constructive ideas into consciousness while you are fearing dreaded ones. Try to imagine a cool, peaceful swim on a hot day at the same time as you are imagining the exhaustion and agony of drowning. It cannot be done. These two kinds of image-building are as opposite as night and day, and they cannot function together in the mind at one time.

To put it another way, our emotional energy may be invested in either hope or fear. When hope energy is projected outwardly into the world, it unifies peoples and builds civilizations. When fear energy is projected into the world, it sows the seeds of conflict and undermines civilization. Thus hope and fear displace each other, completely and mutually, in both inner and outer space.

Einstein observed that no problem can be solved at the level at which it was created. The nuclear weapons problem was created from the fear of being weak. But the weapons only make us weaker and more vulnerable to destruction. The solution to the problem seems to involve the contradiction of shifting our attention *away* from missiles and vulnerability, and *towards* what we want in their place. We must stop worrying about the Russians and their bombs, and *fill our minds* with the urgency to achieve a community of interests with them, a community so interdependent and mutually essential that "the problem", having been displaced by a secure and profitable relationship (such as exists between the states of the Union), withers away from inattention.

The filling of our minds with this intention involves a *decision to want* — to really, ardently *want* a political objective, which is rather a foreign idea to most of us. We do not usually *decide* when or what to want: wants simply arise in us.

Though as individuals we tend to proceed from what we want rather than from what we might wish to avoid, it is so automatic that it is difficult to demonstrate.

Consider, for example, the efficiencies involved in the problem of finding a dry place to camp in the woods on a rainy night. One does not approach it by trial and error, saying "Well, we can't pitch the tent in the river; we can't pitch it in the mud . . .", and so on, eliminating all the wet places one sees in the hope of eventually stumbling upon a dry one. What we do instead is to imagine the goal or the objective (a dry place) and then start searching for it: for a large sheltering tree or for an overhang. In the cold and the rain it is easy to be motivated by a clear objective, and to be rational and efficient in the pursuit of it.

The point of this analogy is to demonstrate the importance of *how* we frame problems. Finding a dry place *includes* avoiding all the wet places, but avoiding the wet places is not *how* we find the dry one. By the same token, achieving international security must include the avoidance of weakness, but a race to avoid weakness is not *how* we will achieve that security. True security must be based upon agreement, which in turn must be founded upon self-interest, just as the internal security of the states of the U.S. and the provinces of Canada rests upon agreement and mutual self-interest. And whether we like them or not, it is obviously in our best interests to be secure with the Russians; they hold our lives in the palm of their hands, just as we do theirs.

In international affairs the simplicity of this approach to the threat of annihilation is obscured for the individual by the many voices which are speaking from power: from the government, from the military establishment, from the press, from the defense industry, and from the universities. The individual, if he is to hope to promote common sense in international affairs, must first clarify himself in relation to three essential insights: 1) an insight into the ultimate source of power and authority between human beings; 2) an understanding of *how to know what he wants* for the world; and 3) an insight into the nature of love and opportunity. These three insights are capable of revolutionizing the individual's concept of himself in relation to the world. They can equip him to think clearly and with authority about his country's political objectives, and to act confidently and effectively as a citizen in pursuing of them.

*   *   *

POWER

From earliest childhood we learn to distinguish the voice of authority, and it is in the smallness and the dependency of childhood that awe for authority is first felt. In this awe for parental authority are mingled the conflicting feelings of love, need, admiration, resentment, and fear.

There is no magic by which this mix of feelings, so natural in the child, should cease to be triggered in adult life by other more powerful or prestigious adults. So unless one consciously works at understanding oneself, these ancient and habitual feelings of smallness towards authority will persist throughout life. And we are all subject to them in varying degrees.

Many otherwise skilled and talented people retain a lifelong sense of smallness in the presence of official authority. It may be seen in over-solicitous respect, or in contemptuous rebellion: both stem from a *feeling*, an age-old feeling that we have been taught to identify as "respect", but which is at heart a feeling of inequality and smallness.

What happens when many millions of people allow these feelings of smallness to be triggered by those who hold "power" and consequently have "authority"? We see millions of people, caught in either resentment or "respect", handing out the money to gorge an insatiable defense industry.

It's the "What can *I* do?" syndrome again. Somebody *else* has the power and the responsibility. "*I*" am yet a child.

Understanding power is one of the defining wisdoms of the mature adult. Those who never explore their instilled reactions to power remain as children, their lives run largely by others, bolstering themselves by either despising power or by blindly respecting it. To be stuck in this perception of power is a form of preventable bondage which in a truly free and enlightened society would be deplored.

Religious questions aside, what *is* the true and proper source of power in a human life? Consider a single man or woman who discovers that he or she can actually forage alone in the bush, or on a South Seas island. From this simple fact it is obvious that at the survival level a person lives by the power and authority of his own natural endowments — in other words, by his strength and his wits.

Every person who enjoys physical and mental health evolved with the physical power to move and do, and with the mental ability to observe and know. This ability to observe and know the *facts* of one's surroundings (on the South Seas island, for example: where the trickle of fresh water flows; where the coconuts grow; where the fish swim among the reefs) is a cornerstone of human existence. And though modern life has undermined our practice and our confidence to some degree, this age-old survival intelligence is still the most precious thing we have. It is the built-in birthright, the natural power and authority of the individual to *look after himself.*

It was from a profound respect for this natural authority of the individual that democratic principles evolved, and were guaranteed and sanctified in constitutional law. But democracy *cannot work* unless this authority is *used* by the individual. Democracy requires that each person observe and know the *facts*, and that each person respect, *above all else*, his own capacity for independent thought and action. And in no case is the business of delegating one's natural authority potentially more dangerous than in allowing others to tell us what the Soviets are like. It is of paramount importance that as individuals we know what the facts *are*, and later chapters contain suggestions on how to find out.

As this question of delegating one's natural personal authority arises continually in everyday life, it would seem well to understand it once very clearly, and then to be forever on guard against its pitfalls.

Among the definitions of "authority" are the "power to influence or persuade resulting from knowledge or experience", and the "claim to be accepted or believed".[1] No well person loses his *right* to authority over any matter which concerns him unless he voluntarily gives it up. This is a point of crucial importance. When I go to an expert or an authority for advice or assistance (a mechanic, an architect, an accountant), I authorize that person to provide knowledge and skill on my behalf. But it is I who select that authority, and I who delegate my own authority to him. All that he can ever do to help me is to recommend or execute a procedure that it is finally up to me to accept or reject. So in the end, I have the ultimate responsibility in all matters that concern me.

The *public* official or authority — be he a Congressman, a policeman, or a general — is engaged, and compensated, to use his position to represent our interests. He is an employee of the community and has contracted to do its bidding. He occupies a privileged position of trust and responsibility.

It is when we see the official as having *power* that things begin to go wrong. Power is a psychological phenomenon which involves a mutually perceived transfer of strength from one party to another. Authorities will accept whatever power is voluntarily accorded to them, and from that position will often contrive to take more. But all the power they have adds up to all the power that is relinquished to them. The master's power *is* the combined power of the slaves that obey him. And in a very concrete sense, all of the ugly, hovering power of the 50,000 warheads in existence is power that the citizens of this planet have negligently allowed to be collected from them. This is a cold, hard, undeniable *fact*. We are all responsible. And there is nothing new in this: every creature in history has carried the responsibility to use its own strength as effectively as possible to achieve its survival. And that survival *is* an achievement, and not guaranteed under warranty, is a point that often escapes attention in our time.

IMAGINATION AND WANTING

We said in the foregoing section that people first delegate their political power upwards, and then feel manipulated by those who take it. The bottom line seems to be that people would rather complain, from a position of supposed weakness, than to think out carefully what they do want, and then intelligently pressure their leaders to deliver it. The middle class is having too good a time to get involved, and the poor are too tired and demoralized. So it is convenient for many of us that in spite of our griping against the government, there are still people "up there" willing to tell us what we should want. This convenience of listening to the authorities is an extraordinarily costly one, though, for it confuses people everywhere about their own centers of wanting, and turns democracy upside down.

The Classic Forces for Change

The message should be obvious: to be worthy of the great institution of democracy, each individual must learn to know his own mind, and to make his own position count. In other words, he must develop his political imagination (which is his capacity to want political ends), and then learn the techniques of non-violent action and conflict resolution.

Learning to focus on what we *want* for the world will involve wheeling our attention around in a one hundred and eighty degree about-face, and opening our minds to the vast, uncharted potential for human community on this planet. This refocusing will mean taking control of the images that we experience internally. Should we succeed in mastering our thoughts, we shall not only quell the current danger, but in so doing we shall establish a new frontier in the evolution of the human species, a frontier, this time, *within* man. And there is nowhere for this transformation to occur in the human species other than within each human being.

How, then, does a person begin to curb his stifled, fearing imagination, and render in its place his unknown, untapped creative potential?

As we suggested before, he must first consciously establish a *clear division* in himself, a division between the thoughts which flow automatically into his head, and the watchful, detached part of himself that can back away and observe these thoughts. In this respect it is useful to liken the images that flow through consciousness to movies that play internally. Some movies (inner sequences) are good: they promote enthusiasm, happiness, energy, plans, and fulfillment. Others are bad, producing worry, tension, apathy, depression, and withdrawal. But if a person remembers that part of himself can back away at any time and take up the role of projectionist, then that remembering part of the self can *select* which movies to play. This has been called "self remembering"[2] or "self-reflective consciousness"[3]. This division in the self allows a person to sit, as if on a safe rock, high and dry in the back of his mind, and decline to be immersed in the storm of the primitive self — in the fear, suspicion, and violence that have so ravaged man.

If the majority of us could locate this capacity within ourselves — could agree to find the rock, so to speak — we could recognize and monitor the storms not only within ourselves, but between one another. If we could further project this principle into international relations, we could replace the culture's habitual thoughts of treachery and suspicion with the steadfast intention of securing world peace. It is ultimately a question of the number of people who will grasp this necessity. Working backwards from where we are headed now, this is *what* we will have learned to do if we end up by escaping the ultimate consequences of our own vestigial violence.[4]

It is time to commit our thoughts, therefore, with a resolute singleness of purpose to a new and life-affirming goal for human civilization. That goal must include recognition of the pure dog-like primitiveness of the enmity that adult human beings indulge in themselves. We must elevate our concerns for human welfare to the entire globe, for we are all the same, and there will always be trouble until we yield to the inescapable fact that we are one species living on one planet. If half the energy dedicated to human conflict (law-suits, divorces, strikes, lock-outs, rapes, murders, tanks, and missiles) could be placed in the service of man's basic needs for food, shelter, clothing, health, and education, there would be no need to waste our lives in bitter struggle against one another.

Why are we not sorting this out? Are struggle, fear and violence the inevitable human condition, or can we evolve as a species to transcend them? When the stakes are high, can we reach yet higher ground within ourselves, and meet together upon it? This is a question in the evolution of individual consciousness, almost a question of the geography of consciousness itself. Let us begin by charting the process of enmity. Consider the two columns below. The left column traces the inner sequences which produce the circle of enmity, and the right column suggests sequences which would neutralize it.

THE CIRCLE OF ENMITY

What We Have	**What We Want**
1. Our own potential for suspicion, doubt, treachery, and violence, which we tend not to recognize when we are immersed in them.	1. To make a clear division between the self that may become immersed in suspicion, doubt, malice, etc., and the objective self that can back away and observe this process.
2. Our conscious recognition of these capacities is reserved for the enemy, upon whom we project the unpleasant qualities we do not wish to see in ourselves: malice, hostility, treachery, etc. We project the source of "the problem" onto him, which allows us to remain "right" and "good".	2. To keep an open mind about the enemy, who may or may not be falling into the trap of projecting his own malice, suspicion, etc. onto us. To be on guard against the habit of wanting to feel "right".
3. Human rightness and goodness is located here, in us; and human wrongness and badness is located over there, in him.	3. To see the struggle between good and evil (or between love and fear) as a universal struggle within every man and woman at the individual level.
4. Thus we cannot see the enemy at all well; what we *do* see is the mirror of our own projected malice, hostility, suspicion, etc.	4. To assess the enemy for how much he is or is not projecting onto us. To lead him out of this projecting behavior.
5. As we cannot see the enemy through our own unconsciously projected suspicions, we become preoccupied with how the enemy is perceiving us, because we have no way of testing him as long as we are confusing ourselves with him.	5. If we are able to really look at the enemy, what we see is his fear of us. If we break the vicious circle of projection first, we will cease to be preoccupied with what we *imagine* to be his perception of us; instead we will be able to observe it firsthand.

107

6. Meanwhile the enemy is doing exactly the same thing, and we are mutually caught between the infinitely reflecting mirrors of unwanted, unclaimed human badness.

6. When we stop mirroring ourselves against the enemy, the vicious circle of mutually projected badness is broken, and there is room for understanding, humor and compassion to enter.

7. Neither side can trust the other to communicate with honesty or integrity, so communication breaks down entirely, and into the vacuum of silence flows more mutually projected distrust and hostility.

7. When there is true receptivity even on one side, the other side becomes immediately alert and hopeful for the relief of improved relations. Into the vacuum of silence flow cautious but constructive dialogue.

8. From this mutual isolation, both sides act out their worst fears, building missiles, shelters, Star Wars, etc., to the point of world-force obliteration.

8. The goal of discussion must be to share common fears and find ways to address them, instead of acting them out through the technology of annihilation.

9. All imagination on *both* sides is caught up *within* "the problem". "An inner situation (that we are all both good and bad) not made conscious, happening outside, as fate." The hostility and treachery we mutually disown in ourselves is projected outward to poison international relations. A phenomenon of mutual alienation, stemming from the undivided self, completes the circle of enmity.

9. All imagination (at least on *one* side) is directed beyond the problem towards desired outcomes. There is no unresolved inner situation (at least on one side) to be acted out as fate, to tear the world asunder. At least one side is in a proper state of internal balance to approach, with good will, the unresolved concerns of the other. One side has acted with courage and intelligence to break the primitive circle of enmity.

The approach in the left column can *never* be solved within its own terms because the problem is one which has been defined and created within the mind, and is therefore by definition illusory. As a political phenomenon, "the problem" is a mass delusion, admitting of no solution from within its point of view.

When we accept the sequences outlined in the left column,

what we are ultimately working on trying to solve is our own projected view of the Soviets, which we are locked into in a mass (and therefore plausible) way. Our perceptions, our imaginings, our mental picture of the Soviets (and they have a variation of this picture of us) is not open to a solution, because it is a fully-accepted, internalized assumption which is regarded as factual and as corresponding to "reality". Our picture of them, and theirs of us, is the first, undermost underpinning in a structure which is inevitably filled with competition, suspicion, provocation, and violence. So the picture creates the reality, and there is no way to defeat the reality while projecting the picture. The resulting problem is logically impossible to solve.

When we approach our relationship with the Soviets not as a "problem" (though our picture does make it *seem* like a problem), but as something which we would like to fashion according to our preferences, then the most desirable view of the matter would be that we become friends with them. But we balk at this because of "the picture". Having the picture firmly in mind as the reality, we dismiss hopes for friendship and understanding as being idealistic, and we thereby sustain the reality, which reinforces the picture, which further sustains the reality, and so on. The world is indeed a mirror.

So if we indeed desire world friendship, open channels of communication, and general peacefulness, can we lose by trying to form a more optimistic picture, and if so, would this picture have the power to influence its object? Most of us have had uneasy relations with a neighbor at one time or another, and the wish to be free of this nearby "heaviness" will often prompt us to take a first step in changing the picture from an unpleasant, nagging hostility into the relaxation and freedom of harmony. Such a gesture proceeds from the inborn sense that all people are fundamentally like ourselves, so that a kind word can hardly fail to tap the "up" side of the other person. If the person (or nation) has experienced undue or prolonged emotional suffering, then the effort may require repetition, but few cases are hopeless.

So a change in our picture of the Soviets, which could begin with a simple speculation as to what they really are like, might free the Soviets from this mutually locked-in perceptual stalemate as much as it would free ourselves.

It is ironic that in projecting dishonesty and untrustworthiness into the enemy we are in fact crediting him with a similarity to ourselves. For if these qualities are not present in us, then how are we able to anticipate them? If we unconsciously feel that the "down" side of the enemy is akin to the "down" side of ourselves, then we must also know that somewhere in both of us there is higher ground on which to meet. And it is in the uniquely human capacity to build constructive images that this higher ground will be found.

LOVE AND OPPORTUNITY

We have suggested that the history of mankind is, most significantly, the history of evolving consciousness. This idea is gaining popular momentum.[5] It is the idea that man embodies the integration of physical and spiritual principles, and that his self-reflective consciousness represents a new frontier in the possibilities for human life on this planet.

We already know that man has achieved remarkable insight into the physical principles which govern his existence. The question is, will he gain a corresponding insight into himself? Until this question can be answered in the affirmative, each day that passes with civilization still intact is a day of reprieve against a lurking extinction. Reprieve after reprieve, as if some soul of life within the planet were waiting for the human brainchild to wake up one morning and love the earth enough *that* day to deliver it from his antics of annihilation. Each day that dawns is above all else a day of opportunity for every person alive to awake from his personal dreams and take his share of a hold on human destiny.

And the measure of our destiny will surely be our capacity to love our lives and the planet we live on. But what determines this capacity for love? And what *is* love?

Love, in all its forms, is an emotional surrender to the beautiful or the exquisite. It is a gladness that touches the soul with wonder, tenderness, sublimity, or joy. Its moments are utterly complete and perfect, lacking in nothing. It is the absolute home of the heart, and it is so precious to human beings that its very existence makes them unspeakably fragile.

Every human spirit carries the inborn promise of the awaiting perfection, the hovering elusiveness of love. In the face of this haunting expectation, man struggles in every direction — through religion, position, possessions, sex, money, and friends — to transcend the incompleteness of his spirit. But how often, admidst all these satisfactions, do those uninvited, unexpected moments of transporting perfection occur?

Perhaps the key to the riddle lies in the fact that such moments are never anticipated. Many highly satisfactory moments are planned, but they are not the same. Planning requires effort and expectation, whereas love is sourceless and effortless. Its sourcelessness, beyond the human will, makes it the province of God, and to receive it is a grace. But one cannot command a grace, or a gift of any kind. It is precisely because gifts are beyond our control that makes them so highly prized.

To receive the grace of love is much more than the sense of *being* loved. Rather it is a movement within the spirit which gives one the sense of *not being anything* apart from a purity of feeling. It is the merging of the spirit with the infinite natural order of the universe, and within that union there is no separateness and no loneliness.

The order of the universe, which can only be perceived through the receptivity of love, cannot be experienced if man is obstructed with ideas of how the universe should be. Any idea of how the world *should* be constitutes a displacement and a rejection of the way it *is*. If the mind is already full of its own desires — like a vessel full of water — it cannot receive anything new or fresh. And if the spirit is already in isolated motion within, it cannot be united with order outside through the subtle rising of love.

In man's efforts to control the universe, therefore, we see the very resistance which denies him the love he craves. And he is particularly resistant to other men, and perhaps understandably so, for it is in mankind that disorder is most apparent. But it helps to remember that the source of man's disorder lies in his separation from love. Man himself is part of the great "what is", and when he is in order he is magnificent.

For mankind to be in order, he must first learn to understand the difference between the images of the world as he would like it to be, which drive him to despair, and the actual world, which is all that can move his love. But he is so entangled in this confusion that the only hope for escape lies in the unraveling power of reason.

In religious terms, the subject at hand is enlightenment, which the mystics tell us is not possible unless it is both desired and consciously pursued. This means that the evolution of love in the individual is a deliberate awakening dependent upon choice and will. The motivating force behind this choice is either love itself, or the painful vacuum left by its absence.

If reason is to untangle the confusion, it should begin by asking what it is that preoccupies the mind and displaces the spirit of love. We suggested before that the mind is full of ideas of how things should be, or of how we would *like* them to be. We continually hold these ideas up to reality, find that reality does not correspond, and then reject the reality. We are left with the *ideas* intact, but with residual disappointment and resentment toward *the truth*.

But where do these ideas come from — these phantom standards by which we judge the real? They are expectations derived from the past. They are our beliefs, values, attitudes, tastes, manners, and fears, and what they cannot include is love, for love is the unifying merger with the present.

Every head carries around its own unique past. Beliefs and values are instilled through cultural lineage and training: it is "good" to be honest, clean, punctual, kind, and generous. It is "bad" to lie, cheat, be late, lazy, hateful, and miserly. Standards of manners and dress are also imbibed through the culture. Fears are both cultural and personal. If a dog bit me when I was four years old, I cannot look at a dog without that memory and without a corresponding reaction to all present dogs.

In this way we traverse life *full* of the past, and through it all we judge the present. We cannot look upon a barking dog, a wrongly-held fork, a loud necktie, or an unmowed lawn without an inner movement of rejection. Similarly, we feel obliged to approve, respect, and admire those who demonstrate the virtues that we have been trained from childhood to portray. But respecting people is not the same as loving them. Is it any wonder that we are so infrequently capable of being moved, from an empty quietude of mind, to simple, unifying love?

So the order of the inner sequence is thus: belief (or value), judgement, rejection, isolation, lovelessness, meaninglessness, and despair. Not a huge, all-encompassing despair, but little despairings that punctuate the hours and the days. And how they add up! Open any newspaper on any day and see what trouble the world is in. Most of this trouble originates in preconceived ideas of what people think they need, not from necessity itself.

But let us get back to unraveling the dilemma. Having understood the enormous cultural barriers to love, suppose a person decides to take them on. Though he may continue to live by the practical values of his own upbringing, he decides to quiet the internal buzz of his cultural soundtrack. He resolves to monitor himself for bias, and to catch himself in the acts of rejection and denial. This entails a total commitment to a continuing process of self-transformation. But such a commitment cannot be sustained unless it is firmly grounded in meaning.

So the old question arises, "what is the meaning of life?" Some people are lucky enough to discover, from their own centers of observation and authority, that nobody has the answer, that it is not written in the heavens, and that it only really exists in man's head, as a belief. So the course is wide open and free. The meaning of life is something people may choose to define for themselves; they may become, in effect, the architect of meaning and quality in their own lives. "What is the meaning of life?" becomes "What meaning do I wish to live for?"

The form this question takes is vastly significant to personal destiny. It makes a strategic difference to whether a person lives at the cause or at the effect of the circumstances of his life. The instant the question is reformulated, choice appears on the scene, and the bonds of determinism dissolve to release the creativity of free will.

Because the decision to cultivate one's capacity for love is an *act of conscious will*, it cannot occur without full intention. It is the most significant choice a human being can make, and the most spiritually strengthening as well.

Nor does it blind a person to suffering and despair. As a state of receptivity which displaces despair, love provides the courage and the wisdom to lead others out of the jungle of negative emotion. And whether people dwell in negativity through experience or temperament, they can always be encouraged towards the quietness of mind which is conducive to love, and towards the realization that they may will this state of mind for themselves. They can be taught to back away from their habitual stance, and to ask the question, "Do I really *prefer* to endure this frustration?" If the answer is "no", then change is on the way. And the more people who choose to live for all that is or could be lovely or beautiful on this planet, the better off everyone will be.

When a person decides to live from his center of love, it grows in the light of the reflections it brings. As the quality of this center develops, happiness becomes less random, less conditional, and less subject to external influences. The decision to travel through life in love is therefore essentially a practical one: it is the single act of volition which gives a person the greatest control over the quality of his consciousness, whatever discomforts may happen to intrude.

To actively love life then, is first to observe the orderliness and harmony of the natural world; then to discover that in man's unique suspension between order and chaos there lies choice; and finally to seek order in oneself. One then becomes capable of living harmoniously in the world and of helping others to do the same.

The infinite mind-boggling orderliness that the mind of man tracks during his explorations of particle physics, biochemistry, astronomy, oceanography, and the human body itself — this profound order at the heart of all things has been attributed by mystics to God. As the mind of man follows the mind of God, he experiences reverence, gratitude, and love. And these are just the emotions which will protect the planet from man's lower, unawakened self.

Let us turn now to our present disorder. Consider the diagram below. The thing we have that contains all else is, of course, our existence, our lives — and our lives are supported by this orderly planet we have been discussing. Within these lives we give time and energy to life's requirements and satisfactions, promoting all that we can in the way of happiness and security for ourselves and our loved ones. But what good is individual security when our existence itself is so threatened? Surely we must attend to planetary security first, and then get back to doing what we were doing within the circle of existence in the diagram. Obviously we cannot just drop everything, but even if the average person were to commit an hour each week to the issue of planetary security, the situation would be vastly improved.

Diagram 5.
The Circle of Being or Existence,
Which Contains Daily Life.

We know that the danger of nuclear war is the gravest danger humanity has ever faced — or more to the point, has ever declined to face. Perhaps what stops us from facing it is a paralysis we feel in relation to crisis.

The Chinese have a language character for "crisis" — "wei chi" — which means, at the same time, both "danger" and "opportunity". To us in the West who see crisis as synonymous with danger, this can be an instructive pairing of concepts. A word which links danger to opportunity not only takes some of the alarm out of a crisis, but even suggests prospects for improvement. "Wei chi" implies that though attention and awareness are required to overcome danger, the act of overcoming it produces the confidence and exhilaration that lead in new directions.

Eastern language and thought are full of such cultural insights into life's underlying dualities. Everything contains its opposite, and balance, proportion, and natural order are seen at the heart of all spiritual and physical things. What has been institutionalized in Eastern language is a kind of built-in faith in the reasonableness of life, a faith that tempers fear, which as we have been saying is the greatest enemy of mankind. So wisdom and faith go hand in hand, and both are the fruit of receptive observation — the receptive observation of love.

If the nuclear crisis is a case of "wei chi", it may well present an opportunity proportionate to its danger, but do we have the wisdom to recognize it, or the faith to see it?

If the nuclear crisis contains both danger and opportunity, then surely the opportunity is to choose global unification over the threat of extinction. The danger is that we will fail to adapt to the new terms of our existence. These terms are that unless we overcome the primeval use of force as the arbiter of disputes, it will annihilate us. The opportunity, on the other hand, is that we renounce violence as obsolete and evolve into superior beings — a prize which seems commensurate with the horror of the inferno. In some uncanny way we have entered the metaphor of the choice between heaven and hell.

So while the earth is yet green and the skies deep blue, and while the young of all creatures dance with new life, there is still the opportunity to turn our spaceship Earth on a course towards survival. But to become master of the ship the human species must first transform itself. A great change of heart and a wave of determination must sweep up through the general population. And leaders who have been standing in the way of peace[6] must bow to a people who wish to live harmoniously on their earth — to a people who refuse to gamble the gift of life in a hideous game of nuclear roulette.

But the people are slaves to the roulette croupiers, and they will remain so until they understand *themselves*. Until then their fears will be constantly aroused by those in whom fear is uppermost — by those who seek relief from anxiety through power and the primitive law of force. Such desperate men will rule the earth until people no longer buy their views. And buy them we do, to the tune of billions. It is up to all of us to get down to our own cases, now, and earnestly, to ensure that at least within our own spheres of influence the images of hope, trust, and compassion will prevail.

Part IV

Acting

CHAPTER 10

THE QUALITY OF ALIVENESS:
Having Something to Lose

This fourth and final section of the book deals with solutions. It contains conflict resolution techniques and an inventory of citizen strategies which are available to people everywhere who wish to use their weight to tip the planetary scales towards peace.

Wishing to act, wishing even to see the scales tipped, implies that one has something at stake, something important to lose by merely standing back and waiting for the bomb. And in action itself there is an implicit confidence, an expectation that one *can* be effective, that one *can* make a difference.

Both these things — having something to lose, and feeling strong and effective — boil down to one's essential vitality. They come down to the bedrock base from which we all think, feel, and act: our health.

When the body is fresh, tuned, and invigorated, a person is comfortably grounded in *feeling good*. He is in touch with the great flow of energy which is the natural condition of a healthy body. To actively use the body, to feel its strength and aliveness, is an emotional and a spiritual experience as well. To be regularly grounded in the body's physical strength is to feel power, confidence, and optimism. This basic aliveness is the underlying force of our existence, and it cannot be threatened without a vigorous reaction.

Yet man faces annihilation without demonstrating this reaction. We have already explored some of the psychic blocks which contribute to this phenomenon; now we shall question the quality of our physical well-being. Is it good enough that we have something vital to lose?

There is a widespread cultural confusion in the West concerning the nature of physical well-being. Take, for example, the matter of food. For centuries mankind has struggled against the soil and the elements to overcome the chronic scarcity of food. Throughout history he has rejoiced in times of plenty, with the feast as a symbol of victory over the background hardship of life.

In the short time since the Great Depression of the 1930's, however, the average North American has achieved an unparalleled, unprecedented control over "the good life". But in spite of this recent freedom from hardship, the triumph of the feast remains.

Having decades past secured life's basic needs, North Americans have turned their attention to embroidering their daily bread into a thrice-daily art form. As general prosperity has risen, the focus of the good life has beamed increasingly on gourmet cooking and international cuisine — from souvlaki to teriyaki, from burritos to curry, from fondue to pasta to tapas to schnitzel.

Visitors to the country are dazzled by the spectacular bounty of its supermarkets. In response to the nation's epicureanism, these showcases have laden their shelves with fresh, out-of-season fruits and vegetables; with exotic foreign condiments and spices; with endless varieties of meats and cheeses, and with countless tinned, bottled, and packaged delicacies. And to enhance every conceivable gourmet delight, the liquor shelves abound with the requisite bordeaux, vermouths, cognacs, ports, whiskies, and brandies. No stone is left unturned as America feasts from every culinary tradition in the world.

Eating out has become a national diversion. The steak and egg breakfast, the champagne brunch, the three-martini lunch, the happy hour, and the after-movie snack. McDonald's. The ubiquitous Italian, Greek, Chinese, Mexican, French, Japanese, and

East Indian restaurants, all complete with cocktails, truck-stop portions, Spanish coffee, and doggybags.

Three meals a day have become three excursions into the ruminating sublime. Working to live, and living to eat — as artistically, as frequently, and as abundantly as possible.

To offset this sheer volume of intake are the diet soft drink industries, the no-fat yoghurts, the non-sugars, and the no-cholesterol dressings. And, while much of America is hugging itself with delight over tonight's chapter in the good life, the evening news is panning today's chapter in world famine, pausing to study the deep-set, patient, and unreproachful eyes of starving children.

America, with 6% of the world's population, is consuming 40% of the world's resources. This rising tide of overconsumption is challenging the nation's health as effectively as the defeated old killers — smallpox, diptheria, cholera, plague, typhoid fever, and tuberculosis. Today's killers are the avoidable diseases of lifestyle and choice.

We have gradually been evolving, and are beginning to take for granted, some extreme and contradictory behaviors. While many are enduring the fast lane of corporate stress on the one hand, countless others are passively swaying through life under a burden of obesity on the other. The stress, the smoking, the chronic inactivity, the overweight, the refined foods, and the dietary fats are combining to produce epidemic levels of heart disease, high blood pressure, and cancers of the lung and bowel.

These excesses of over-indulgence run counter to our rugged cultural heritage, which may help to explain the epidemic level of demoralization — the guilt, anxiety, insomnia, depression, suicide, sexual identity problems, and alcoholism.

These problems often stem from disorders of self-esteem. Any form of self-esteem, high *or* low, arises from a self-image that is carried in the mind. This image is a picture which is projected upon the mind's eye, and is therefore an invention. The true, centered, feeling self, on the other hand, is grounded in the body, whose senses connect us to the outside world. It is through the body that we receive life and feel — a cool breeze, a bird on the wing, a hot meal, a pang of alarm, a welling tear, or an embrace.

The preoccupation with self-worth, on the other hand, subordinates the body to the mind's activity, which carries on at the body's expense. The body's messages become obscured by the mind, which in acting out its self-concept is distracted from actually feeling. So the wisdom of the body, which guides us in all of its functions, is lost. We end up with a raft of physical complaints — nervousness, constipation, insomnia, disorders of the eating and sexual appetites — all of which arise from the neglect of the body. To relieve these complaints we reach for every available anesthetic: nicotine, alcohol, valium, librium, heroin, angel dust, and glue. And after a lifetime of denying the body we line up at the hospitals for the open heart surgeries, the transplants, the fat removal, and the bowel resections. In addition to all this trauma and expense, the great failed potential for human health and beauty is a direct result of being cut off from natural feeling.

The ingredients of really feeling good are subtle ones, and require a slowing down of the mind and a receptiveness to the actual physical sensations of the moment. In contrast to this slow, savoring, appreciative kind of awareness, people often think they are feeling good, or are about to feel good, when they are doing something that the culture lauds as desirable, such as feasting.

Examples abound. Most of our food is artificially salted, and when salt is left out the standard reaction is that the food lacks flavor. This is a cultural bias, and one which causes epidemic high blood pressure. When people are forced by health problems to omit the salt, they begin to realize, with some wonderment, that for years the rather harsh and burning sensation of salt has been masking the subtle and intriguing flavor of simple food. For the first time they discover the true taste of cereal, of butter, of peas. Within days the reintroduction of salt is experienced like a harsh, glaring light, overilluminating the food and uniformly blanketing its wonderful sweetness and variety. It is worthwhile to realize that all food takes up salt from the soil, as do all the animals who graze that food, and that we in turn evolved by eating very little salt.

Another impediment to the true appreciation of food is eating too frequently. Only when hunger dictates the timing of meals does a person fully experience the remarkable sweetness of natural foods. Personally speaking, I have occasionally fasted for a few days, and once broke a fast by eating some cooked garden peas. It was easily the most delicious taste I have ever experienced — it was the *magnified essence* of the sweetness of peas! It is very likely that the poor people of the earth gain more true pleasure and contentment from their food than do the new Romans of America, with all their plentitude.

The confusion between thinking one feels good and actually feeling good is classically demonstrated by the smoker, whose mind's conditioning prevails over the subtle protests from the body. The smoker believes that he is addicted to nicotine, and at the slightest emotional tension or discomfort he yearns to fill the hollow in his lungs with the fullness of smoke. After a deep breath or two he is relieved: he relaxes and settles down.

In actual fact the cigarette is blunting his consciousness and taking the edge off his awareness by depriving him of oxygen. And though he is experiencing subjective relief, his physical stress level is actually increasing through a rise in blood pressure and heart rate.

If a smoker really wants to explore his own body's rejection of inhaled tobacco, he should tune himself to feel, as objectively as possible, all that happens as he smokes his first cigarette of the day.

Yes, the empty craving in the lungs is relieved, and that is where the smoker's attention is primarily focused. But at the same time an ever-so-fine curtain of dullness descends to blunt the sharpness of the mind. If he focuses attention on his limbs, he may notice a subtle, rather discouraging heaviness seeping into his arms and legs as they, too, are deprived of oxygen. He may even feel a suggestion of nausea. But the focus of his craving is too narrow to notice that he is not, in fact, feeling *good*. A cigarette cannot make him feel really good, though it does stop him from feeling the hunger of its own gnawing addiction.

It is much the same with alcohol, a habit which in moderation is far less harmful than smoking. But alcohol, with all its glow and social charm, draws that same veil of dullness across the mind, robbing the senses of their immediacy and taking the sparkle and freshness out of a clear day.

What we have been exploring here is the difference between feeling good and "feeling no pain". If you were to attempt to measure them, feeling good would be measured on a positive scale, starting from zero, while feeling the relief of yielding to addiction would be measured by the reduction in a negative scale.

The same kind of measurement could be applied to all compulsive habits, from overeating, to overworking, to promiscuity. This base, this touchstone of what we mean by feeling good, is relative to the experience of each individual — and everyone is locked into the limitations of his own experience. Each individual has assessed his degrees of well-being within the relativity of his own experience, and is therefore oblivious to the possibilities which lie beyond.

At this point I would like to recount a dream I had about three years ago, which transported me beyond the limitations of my previous experience, and in doing so changed the course of my life. It even led, eventually, to the writing of this book.

I was in my late thirties at the time, in good health, and walking about four miles a day. I was about twelve pounds overweight, and reasonably satisfied with my physical condition.

Then one night I had a vivid dream which I shall never forget. In the dream I was young (but not small), and light, and running like the wind. I was running as lightly and easily as an antelope, gliding past the evergreens, the lawns, the gardens, and the roses of an old country estate remembered from childhood. As I ran so freely and effortlessly I was somehow blended into the natural beauty and greenery of the place, so that finally I was aware only of motion itself — of trees approaching and sliding by on either side, and there was the exhilaration of total escape from the earthbound heaviness of the body.

I awoke with the magical feeling of the dream floating about me, and it stayed with me for much of the following day. But by contrast I became aware of the realities of my condition: of the roll around my midriff that hampered bending, and of the sloppy tendons around my knees and ankles that cried out at sudden movement. In short, I realized, I had lost my youth, and its re-markable presentation to me of the night before shone out as something past and glorious and beyond reach.

For some months afterwards I went on in the old way, but the memory of the dream would return, and with it a growing desire to recapture that light, effortless feeling of the running, of disap-pearing from myself to enter the landscape.

I decided to find out what was possible for me. I began slowly (cautioned by friends in the fitness business not to overdo it by expecting too much) to work up to the point where I could run several consecutive miles every other day. And though for the first few weeks the run was initially a little gruelling, I *always* felt invigorated afterwards. The run would produce a kind of in-ner cleanness, a freshness of the body akin to sleeping between new sheets.

It soon became clear that I had established a new standard of well-being for myself, and that if I missed my run for a few days an uneasy sluggishness and irritability would descend upon me — the very condition, presumably, that I had taken for granted for so many years, while claiming to be "feeling good". So I had entered another dimension of health, one that I would not have discovered without the dream.

Running produces a whole spectrum of life improvements which its devotees delight in sharing with one another, and in urging upon their reclining friends. But before going into these, I hasten to add that for those who cannot run, other forms of continuous rhythmic exercise will serve as well, if they are performed regularly, and continuously elevate the heart. These include cycling, swimming, skipping, rowing, cross-country skiing, canoeing, and kayaking. It is not recommended, however, to launch upon an exercise program without first consulting a doctor, a fitness specialist, or one of the many good books on the subject. A partial list of these books is contained in Appendix II.

The first dividend of fitness is a new and ever-present awareness of the *physicalness* of the body. It is important to go into this, because the hurdles involved in getting started can defeat people unless they have a really clear image of the rewards which, once attained, they will not want to be without.

Exercise is the stretching and flexing of the muscles, and as the muscles are bought to life by the blood coursing through them, they freshen and tingle with pleasure. This pleasure is one of nature's finest gifts, and is abundantly evident in animals — observe the charging about of a horse or a dog, glorying in the strength and freshness of its limbs. Once this use of the body begins, the muscles start to demand their pleasure, almost to crave this simple stretching, without which they feel confined, restricted, and tight. This subtle anticipation of the body to be stretched and used is present as a continuous feeling of imminent aliveness. It is the backdrop to the day, and it subliminally tips one's disposition towards optimism, enjoyment, and fun.

Exercise is also an effective safety valve against stress. Modern life runs at a pace which besieges the body with urgent demands; hour after hour the body is geared up by adrenalin to fight or take flight. At the end of a hard day the mind is racing, the muscles tense and aching, and the spirit numb with fatigue. But if one runs before dinner, the pressure just blows out of the system, like steam escaping from a boiler, and one returns home refreshed and alive again.

A martini or a tranquilizer, on the other hand, simply blunts the awareness of these stored-up tensions; instead of being released they remain in the body like a coiled spring. Life becomes a contest against tension — weight goes on, blood pressure rises, and the pleasure of the body is buried under a cloak of anesthesia. Is it any wonder there is so much resentment and bickering, so many broken marriages and teenage suicides, in a culture full of rushed, sedentary people? Would the depressions and heart problems and cancers persist so stubbornly in a society which listened to the body as well as to the mind?

It is time for North America to mature into its extravagant wealth; to look in the mirror and take stock of its actual condition. There is evidence to suggest that this is happening already, and in many quarters. As the ancient battle against scarcity has largely been won, the primitive impulses of hoarding and overeating are being put to one side. A new perspective is emerging, and awareness is focusing upon the nutrition and lifestyle habits that actually *feel* best.

In this respect the country remains split, polarized between two extremes. On the one hand are the fat cats, who have lost their will and are following the course of least resistance into heaviness, inactivity, and self-disgust. But on the other hand, and in obedience to a welcome and fruitful self-control, are literally millions of joggers, swimmers, tennis players, skiers, walkers, and surfers. These people constitute a huge health subculture within the country, and are exerting a growing demand for whole grains, fresh vegetables, and "no-additives" upon the food market. They are living proof that in the face of copious plenty human beings are not merely creatures of surfeit and satiety, like caged animals. Human beings have dignity and choice, and in growing numbers people are choosing the affirming vitality of a disciplined health. This element of choice is new, and takes some learning and adapting, whereas in former times the majority were automatically disciplined by circumstance — by economic scarcity, lack of transportation, and hard work.

Within this new health subculture, Americans are giving up smoking and lowering their heart disease. They are eating less refined foods and are running with their children. If this current trend towards feeling well continues to expand, it would seem to follow that the heavy, pessimistic, death-ridden decadence of nuclear weapons will become intolerably repugnant towards ordinary people. It is, at any rate, an avenue for hope.

There is no shortage of encouragement and assistance available for anyone who is fed up with his or her own round shoulders, slack muscles, overweight, and fatigue. It is never too late. Anyone who has been succumbing to the down side of "the good life" can, at any time he so wills, take hold of himself and change direction. But first he must see himself in a new light, in the light of what might be *possible* for him.

Here I return to my dream, and my initial misinterpretation of it as a symbol of lost youth. That was a real mistake, which I now, over forty, recognize. Fitness and well-being are not the monopoly of youth. Quite the opposite is true: youth lasts for as long as fitness and well-being can be attained. They are available to everyone whose basic health is sound. We all carry the potential for a richer, stronger, and happier life, but its achievement depends upon the will. The will, in turn, is born from the imagined state of actually *being* there, and in my case this was gratuitously presented in a dream — a fortuitous dream of precognition.

The initial motivation is the important thing, for once started, the movement itself and the feeling good provide ample motivation in themselves. So though it may look like a long haul from square one, this brief period of exercise soon becomes one of the finest and most eagerly awaited parts of the entire day.

Fitness is an industry, and advice on getting started abounds. The country is awash with fitness centers, diet clinics, weight control programs, saunas, heart attack recovery regimes, health food stores, smoking cessation programs, and massage parlors. In seeking help it is important to find reputable and informed assistance. When in doubt, consult an impartial authority such as a health department, a doctor, or a school fitness instructor.

Thousands of books and magazines also claim to point the way. Some of these are excellent, many are hit and miss, and others are downright dangerous. Appendix II of this book contains a list of reading materials which are responsibly written and based upon sound and established principles of diet and exercise.

We only live once, as far as we know. To make the *best* of our lives we need a strong, cleanly running physical machine. Whether young, middle-aged, elderly, or disabled (and there are references in Appendix II which deal with geriatric and handicapped recreation activities), this one time around can be enhanced through physical vitality. Too many people look back from a prematurely squandered health upon lives of lost opportunity. Too late in the day they mourn the preventable early decline and the lost years ahead.

And if a sooner, nuclear death should arrive to cancel our futures, to claim the prize of life from our grasp, will this too indicate a tragic failure to love our lives and make the best of them? Perhaps the gift of life is not an automatic three score ten; perhaps it must be earned — perhaps it must be cherished, with gratitude, and cared for.

*   *   *

To cherish the gift of life is to wish ardently to secure it, yet in the nuclear age no country is secure unless others are secure also. Security is a mutual affair, not a unilateral one. This fact makes it essential that the outmoded concepts which drive the arms race — ideas of "superiority" and "margins of safety" — be replaced with the newer art of principled negotiation or conflict resolution.

This art had its first modern expression through the writings, teachings, and actions of Mahatma Gandhi, who believed that no person or party in conflict ever had a complete monopoly on the truth of that conflict. Antagonists could, by definition, have only a partial grasp on the truths brought to a conflict — one that was largely determined by their own perspective.

In Gandhian terms, truth simply means whatever "is". That which exists. That which exists has reality, or life to it. He held that truth was the highest principle, and that the greatest good was the affirmation of the truth of life itself. Thus, in any *conflict* situation, the truth was the sum-total of that which was true for everyone. Finding it mutually required that each side had the opportunity to see all of the other's points of view.

Gandhi valued conflicts because they provided just this opportunity to see the truth from all points of view. Conflict had the function of raising two contending sides above their limited perceptions of the partial truth into an expanded awareness of the whole truth. This involved forging a third and higher truth which encompassed both perspectives, with harmony as the result. As one Gandhian has described the process, "Gandhian fights are not ordinary fights. Nobody wins until everybody wins . . ."[1]

Gandhi's classic process of finding the truth is called "*satyagraha*", from "*satya*", "that which is", and "*graha*", "to hold fast to". This and newer methods of conflict resolution will be discussed in greater detail in Chapter 12.

In Chapter 11, however, we must first face a dilemma which plagued Gandhi throughout his entire political life: how was one to be perceived by the opponent as strong if one was unwilling to resort to the use of force?

As we have seen, the use of force has been rendered obsolete by nuclear weapons, so our current question too, is, how does one gain the respect of an opponent who still believes in the use of force while you do not?

Gandhi was morally opposed to coercion on the grounds that it permits no options to the opponent other than those intended by the one who applies force. He saw coercive force as a form of violence which denies the opposition freedom of choice and thus prevents an enduring and harmonious outcome.

Gandhi did, however, make a vital distinction between the force which coerces an opponent to choose against his will, and the force that encourages an opponent to examine the two points of view through *satyagraha* and then make a just and right decision from his own free choice. This latter force was based on moral strength and a faith in human nature. Its power lay in the withdrawal of cooperation from a "stronger" opponent whose force it wished to resist.

The Western peace movement is involved in what may be seen as a two-stage operation towards the goal of bilateral nuclear disarmament. The first stage involves bringing its own governments into dialogue internally with the peace groups. This means bringing Western nuclear nations to the bargaining table with their own electorates, and there reaching agreement on the goals and schedules for nuclear arms reductions.

The second stage is for determined Western governments to *achieve nuclear arms reductions* by completing the *satyagraha* process with the Soviets.

At the present time, Western governments do not appear to be seriously committed to an immediate, effective, and lasting arms reduction program. Nor do they seem to respect the wishes or determination of the peace movement. The next chapter (and its appendix) provides a catalogue of the political tools that are unfortunately needed to bring Western democratic nuclear powers into alignment with the interests of both their own citizens and the world at large.

CHAPTER 11

ARMS REDUCTION:
The Politics of Nonviolent Action

Suppose, for the sake of argument, that all eligible voters in the United States had committed themselves to work one hour a week for the prevention of nuclear war. The effectiveness of such a mass grass-roots action would be greatly enhanced if there were a consensus as to what practical steps the U.S. Government should take to lessen the danger. Indeed, it is important that public pressure take forms other than criticism, which in itself offers nothing to constructive leadership. Public pressure should also advance some simple, widely-acclaimed proposals for government action.

It is not possible for unified grass-roots proposals to emerge, however, unless the public has access to the most telling, meaningful facts about the arms race. But the facts are not as newsworthy as are the posturings, provocations, and propoganda statements that issue from the pro-military forces on either side. And while the facts that are leading us down a road to almost certain destruction remain largely ignored, endless chat over sensational, superficial news wins the day around the coffee tables of the nation.

One fact is that the North American way of life is the material success story of all time: that the billions directed to military spending are the gravy left over after the vast majority of people have helped themselves to household appliances, T.V.'s, videos and stereos, and of course, the ubiquitous automobile. The Soviet Union has only one-tenth as many automobiles as the United

States, yet Soviets number 280 million compared to 241 million Americans. The Soviet gross national product of $1.9 trillion is less than one-half of the U.S. $3.9 trillion, which means that if the Soviets *are* keeping up in the arms race, it is costing them twice as much per capita as it costs Americans. It means that Soviet participation in the arms race spells the real sacrifice of consumer goods at the personal level, nationwide. It means that if we, a society already saturated with consumer goods, up the ante with Star Wars, they, struggling within the Communist ideology to match our weapons technology, will be foregoing even more of "the good life" to keep up militarily.

But *are* the Soviets keeping up militarily? According to the U.S. Center for Defense Information in Washington, D.C.,[1] America possesses both more numerous and more modern nuclear weapons across the board (except for Soviet superiority in the rather vulnerable land-based ICBM department) than does the Soviet Union. And while it may be argued that the Soviets have a greater nuclear megatonnage, the new trend towards smaller weapons in the United States is being confidently pursued as a result of vastly improved accuracy in delivery systems. The large early weapons were designed to compensate, via sheer size, for possible failures to hit on target. The U.S. is now dismantling these old models and using the materials to build smaller more numerous warheads of pinpoint accuracy, while the Soviets lag behind with the older technology.

So we in the West built and used the first bombs, we stayed well ahead until the 1970's, and now we have a superior computer electronics industry fueled by the unparalleled energy and resourcefulness of capitalist competition. Where does this leave the military claim (according to the Center for Defense Information) that we must build another 17,000 weapons by 1990 if we are to keep up with the Russians? Who is making this claim, and why?

The answer is that no coherent intelligence is planning this spiral, nor any particular logic guiding it. It is simply happening, and it is out of control. Man's natural curiosity beckons the scientist to new discoveries; his love for precision and technology challenges the engineer to build the weapons systems; and his zest for competition drives the military to deploy them. The Russians are simply the excuse for all this fascination, just as we are the excuse for them. The point is — and everybody knows it — that we must turn it all around before there's a ghastly accident. This is the single most obvious truth about the arms race — that it must be turned around — and it is this knowledge that should be the cornerstone of a massive public proposal to be pressed upon Western governments.

It will be argued, of course, that intensive efforts have been and are being made to achieve arms reductions through negotiations with the Soviets. This brings us to some other rather startling facts that have not been particularly newsworthy.

Since 1948, world military expenditures have increased at an average annual rate of 4.5%. Military expenditures have, in constant dollars, increased by 3000% since 1900. There is now as much spent on the potential to kill people worldwide as there is spent on educating people. This spending has spread out laterally from the five countries who could build major weapons in 1945 to about 30 countries who can build them today. This astonishing growth in military budgets has spawned huge military equipment industries which pressure governments towards even greater spending, with the resulting economic trend towards the militarization of the entire planet. The financial strength of this military-industrial complex represents a formidable political force which is ever-present at the elbows of the arms control negotiators.

For example, during the period of the Strategic Arms Limitation Talks (SALT) and the Vladivostok Accord (1969-1975), the number of deployed strategic launch vehicles increased by one-third. The "successful" Vladivostok negotiations permitted a ceiling of 2640 MIRV's (Multiple Independently Targetable Re-Entry Vehicles) for each side, which was a 217% increase over the existing number at the time. By 1977, the number of independently targetable warheads deployed by the superpowers was four times higher than it was when SALT began.[2] And though the public heart still lightens each time the arms talks are resumed, the fact remains that significant reductions in destructive power have never been achieved in over thirty years. The net result of these talks has been simply an agreement upon the general direction of expansion for one of the fastest growing industries on earth.

This failure of arms control talks is not just a problem of vested interests, or a lack of true intention. There are real difficulties inherent in the process of trying to work out, *in advance*, how to mutually proceed to limit arms. For example, the talks focus attention on the inequalities that exist between the superpowers in relation to their different weapons systems. The tendency is for each side to rush to catch up with the other's strengths, and for the stronger in a particular system to push ahead faster so that it can bargain from a "position of strength". Some weapons are actually invented solely for use as "bargaining chips" "to negotiate away" during the talks. Sometimes these bargaining chips, such as the MIRV's, actually develop into serious weapons that are added to the arsenals of both sides.

In the midst of all this it is not easy for the negotiators to resist domestic pressures to promote weapons spending. Furthermore, the Defense Department will often reject a treaty unless it is promised the right to develop more advanced or destructive weapons in exchange. And while the U.S. and Soviet Governments present the appearance of doing all they can to make the world a safer place, what is often happening is simply a "cosmetic" agreement, in which the signatories come to terms which would have suited them anyway — terms which allow an *increase* in the buildup.

Arms Reduction

Working as we are towards a mass grass-roots proposal, two things should now be evident: 1) that the proposal should seek to turn the arms race around; and 2) that treaties, far from reversing the arms race, have seldom failed to actually stimulate it. In the light of this depressing failure of arms treaties, the peace-seeking public requires a constructive action to urge upon its government in the interests of preventing nuclear war. What action can this be?

Imagine two adversaries standing face to face in a room with gasoline up to their knees, each holding a box of matches. Neither would dare to strike even a single match, but each keeps accumulating more matches, and all the while they argue about how many each has, as though it mattered. What is their escape from this compulsion? Clearly there is no amount of talk or signing of agreements that could be one-tenth as effective as the gesture of one man throwing *even one* of his matches out of the window. A perfectly clear and visible action, it reverses the direction of their locked-in expectations, yet it offers no advantage to the other man. (Such a clear and visible action was recently taken by the Soviet Government in the form of its 18-month moratorium — August 1985 - January 1987 — on nuclear weapons testing. This moratorium was unilaterally extended four times in good faith by the Soviets, during which time the U.S. exploded at least 22 nuclear test bombs.)

The key to the analogy is that if one side is to make a first *move* towards reduction, that move must be so clear and visible that it cannot be seriously regarded as a trick.

If the U.S. wished to begin the process of actual arms reduction, it could invite the world press to stand by while it threw out one of its "matches". Being careful to maintain the balance of arms, it could dismantle one or possibly a group of modern prestigious weapons, such as, for example, ten of its strategic bombers, or one nuclear submarine, or perhaps a dozen ICBM's. A Soviet delegation could be invited to monitor the process, as could an objective global arbitrator who was trusted by both sides and enlisted to verify the procedure. A statement could then be made to the world press that X number of American P's, worth Y dollars, had simply been scratched from the race, and that the Soviets were being publicly invited to follow suit by openly removing a weapon or weapons of equal or greater value.

To overcome possible Soviet skepticism, the United States may need to be patient in demonstrating the seriousness of its intent. It may need to submit to Soviet requests for additional verifications, but once the Soviets became convinced of U.S. integrity, how could they fail to be relieved by the turn of events? And would they not lose world respect (as the U.S. has done for failure to follow the moratorium on testing) for declining to reply in kind?

Let us suppose that the process were to begin very cautiously and tentatively. The main thing would be that for the first time in nuclear history purposeful arms reductions would have actually begun. It is clear from history that nothing happens as long as both sides wait for mutually acceptable treaties to be signed and ratified. And even if the perfect total disarmament treaty were to suddenly materialize — signed, sealed, and delivered — it would mean nothing until someone had the faith to begin dismantling weapons.

Thus we arrive at the third point in the mass political proposal to U.S. leadership to prevent nuclear war. The third point is that U.S. leadership must take *action* to initiate disarmament, and that verifications and negotiations *follow* this action rather than preceding it. *Action* is the only dimension of behavior which can reverse the direction of U.S.-Soviet arms expectations. This is a *key* point, the point that talk is cheap and that actions speak louder than words, and our lives now depend upon a groundswell public recognition of this axiom of human behavior.

In summary, then, a strong wave of unified political intention must be directed at American leadership from an aroused and determined U.S. public. This public unity should be based upon three very simple points: 1) the arms race must be turned around; 2) arms reduction treaties do not work; and 3) it is time for the U.S. Government to take visible action — a thing it can do immediately — to reverse the direction of this formidably destructive force.

*   *   *

Let us now turn to the great spectrum of nonviolent action methods, which range from the purely symbolic (included in this chapter) to the limits of intervention and non-cooperation (listed in Appendix IX). There are possibilities here for anyone who would like to personally intervene in the world's nuclear destiny, no matter what his or her walk in life might be.

For those who simply wish their opposition to nuclear weapons to be seen and counted, there are a wide range of *symbolic* acts of peaceful opposition to government defense policies. Though these serve only as a weathervane of strong public opinion, democratic governments are responsive to clearly voiced mass public concerns.

Mr. Gene Sharp, in part two of his excellent book on nonviolent action,[3] has identified about 50 methods of nonviolent protest and persuasion, for which very brief summaries are detailed below:

1. Public speeches, formal addresses, and religious sermons all provide opportunities to present opinions, intentions, and possible solutions to the nuclear stalemate.

2. Letters of opposition or support, signed by individuals or groups, may be sent to key political figures, and may even be published as "open" letters in newspapers or journals.

3. Declarations by organizations and institutions may be published or read openly to advertise the official positions of

churches, trade unions, volunteer groups, professional associations, and so on.

4. Signed public statements addressed to the general public are commonly presented by occupational and professional groups, such as IPPNW (International Physicians for the Prevention of Nuclear War) to broadcast the position of the body concerned.

5. Declarations of indictment or intention (which include the Declaration of Independence) may be dramatically effective in firing the public imagination and resolve.

6. Group or mass petitions may be signed by large numbers of people who seek to redress a common grievance.

7. Slogans, caricatures, and symbols, displayed in public places, create familiarity with and sustain awareness of the nuclear issue in relation to government policy.

8. Banners and posters may be effectively displayed during the public addresses of nuclear apologists. When merchants are united in common concern, whole streets of store windows may exhibit such posters.

9. Leaflets, pamphlets, and books may be distributed in the streets, the workplace, and in mailboxes. People of means could purchase stocks of books outlining alternatives to nuclearism and distribute them freely at fairs, festivals, picnics, ballgames and meetings.

10. Newspapers and journals may be started by local or national groups wishing to broaden their base of support. Existing newspapers and journals may accept informative articles and advertisements.

11. Recorded songs, and radio and TV broadcasts are far-reaching vehicles for messages conveying information, concern, and peaceful approaches to world tensions.

12. Skywriting and earthwriting are highly visible media. Earthwriting beneath flight routes may be used by large landowners to display the nuclear disarmament symbol or the dove, either by

ploughing them, or by planting contrasting crops or trees.

13. Deputations of groups or individuals may be sent to see government, United Nations, military, and industrial officials; or to international disarmament and test ban conferences to offer support and encouragement for peaceful solutions.

14. To expand public awareness of those who profit from nuclear roulette, mock awards may be publicly presented to pro-nuclear vested interest groups such as munitions and electronics manufacturers.

15. Repeated group lobbying may be organized by ordinary people to remind senators, congressmen, and Members of Parliament that their constituents are gravely concerned with government commitment to the arms race.

16. Picketing may be conducted in a peaceful non-disruptive fashion around government offices, military installations, and even the White House, as a means of maintaining public pressure while defense issues are being discussed.

17. Mock elections, featuring "polling-places" and "votes" may be held to illustrate public nuclear concerns regarding nuclear weapons, concerns which cannot be realistically voiced during regular federal elections or national referendums.

18. Displays of flags or symbolic colors arouse deep emotion. Black flags are used to denote protest and disapproval, and the beflagging of a whole city during the visit of a President or a Secretary of State can dramatize widespread despondency over the issue of arms escalation.

19. The wearing of symbols, such as a white skull-and-crossbones upon a black armband or headband, appropriately protests the prospect of nuclear death. More constructively, a logo for a nuclear-free planet, such as the sun in a deep blue sky above green fields and a shining sea, could be worn to honor the value of life on our threatened planet. The logo might include a child.

20. Prayer and worship services add spiritual and emotional depth to anti-nuclear demonstrations. They introduce the per-

spective of gratitude for the things that we take for granted, which includes a respect for the "enemy's" right to be different.
21. A grievance may be voiced by delivering symbolic objects to ·an official office. For example, in London in October 1961, Committee of 100 supporters, in protest against Soviet nuclear weapons tests, brought hundreds of bottles marked "DANGER — RADIOACTIVE", in red letters, to the door of the Soviet embassy.
22. Protest disrobings or "nude-ins" emphasize unfair treatment and create media sensation. Their shock value seems mild, however, in comparison to a 30-million degree Centigrade atomic blast.
23. Destruction of one's own property shows marked intensity of feeling against an outrage. The widespread burning of driver's licences for example, would, while demonstrating personal sacrifice, also bring confusion and pressure to bear on municipal and state governments, who in turn would funnel pressure upwards.
24. Imaginative displays of symbolic lights — such as torches, lanterns, candles, and bonfires — demonstrate unity and co-operation amongst people together in the symbolic darkness.
25. Portraits of people such as Bertrand Russell, who symbolize the objective of peace, may be mounted in homes, shops, and public places to aid the collective memory and awareness.
26. Paint may be discriminatingly applied to cover or alter signs or pictures associated with nuclear defense.
27. Signs and names may be newly erected, or erected to replace old ones, to symbolize the objective of peaceful solutions. Street names in campuses, municipalities, industrial parks, and subdivisions might creatively reflect the themes of unity and co-operation. Competitions could be held for original ideas.
28. Symbolic sounds of protest, such as the tolling of church bells in funeral peals, or the baaing of lambs being led to the slaughter, may be eminently suited, on occasions such as the announcements of new defense allocations, to express horror to-

wards the increasing possibility of nuclear holocaust.

29. Symbols of land reclamation — such as the planting of seeds on lands destined for nuclear weapons — suggest the alternative use of the land for constructive domestic purposes.

30. Fraternization with military and other officials who uphold the nuclear order may serve, through friendly contact, to convince them of the grave danger of nuclear policies, and to promote their noncooperation or inefficiency in upholding these policies.

31. Vigils consist of people gathering for long hours in one place, often losing sleep, and showing, with a solemn and religious attitude, their sorrow and consternation over the existing state of affairs.

32. Plays and musical performances expressing the pathos of war can be poignant reminders of the poised fury hanging over us. One of the most moving futility of war songs ever written is "The Green Fields of France", by E. Boyle.

33. Humorous skits and pranks are public vehicles for exposing unrealistic propaganda and arms profits.

34. Singing songs of protest, satire, and hope can express sentiments appropriate to unwanted speeches. They may also be sung during peace walks, vigils, picketing, sit-ins, and rallies.

35. Marches are organized walks to a place which is politically significant to the issue involved.

36. Parades resemble marches, but have no politically significant end point. They seek to express a point of view, often using singing, bands, posters, banners, and leaflets. Centripetal parades start from many locations and converge upon a common center.

37. Religious processions resemble marches or parades, but include the presence of clergymen, the singing of religious songs, and the carrying of religious pictures or symbols.

38. Pilgrimages are long walks, usually lasting days, to a significant destination. They are deeply religious in character, and seek

to alter a morally objectionable condition or policy.

39. Motorcades are slow-driving variations of the march or parade, in which participants tour a larger area with posters, banners, and leaflets.

40. Political mourning employs the symbols of grief for the dead — black clothing, silence, and solemnity — to mourn regrettable political policies or events, such as new deployments of nuclear weapons.

41. Mock funerals grieve the demise of some principle or belief which the demonstrators feel has been violated. Again, the principles of human unity and peaceful co-existence are at odds with nuclear arms racing. Caskets, burning torches, and black flags may be carried to the "graveside".

42. Demonstration funerals are reserved for actual deaths or suicides, and are held in annual sympathy for the victims of Hiroshima and Nagasaki.

43. Graves, such as the Unknown Soldiers, may be visited by individuals or groups as a symbol of moral condemnation towards war. Conversely, the graves of champions of peace and brotherhood may be visited to promote the constructive solutions which are so conspicuously lacking.

44. Assemblies of protest or support may be held outside government offices or around symbolic statues to convey a viewpoint not only to the government, but to the public at large. People may even congregate outside the home of a central figure in the dispute.

45. Protest meetings may be held indoors, or may be mass open-air gatherings with speeches. Such meetings were held during 1961-62 in Trafalgar Square when members of the Committee of 100 were being prosecuted for civil disobedience.

46. Camouflaged meetings of protest are appropriate to regimes in which open meetings are not tolerated, and may include sports events, banquets, and religious, artistic, or other entertainment activities. If Western governments were severely threatened by a massive, determined, unified peace movement, the right to public assembly could be suspended, as was picketing in Britain after the British General Strike of 1926.

47. Teach-ins present a series of speakers to educate the public about the various sides of controversial issues. They encourage questioning of the speakers and discussion from the floor, which helps people to make up their minds and provides a good objective forum for conflict resolution.

48. Silence — obstinate, icy silence — is a powerful tool for conveying public opposition to official announcements presented during meetings, speeches, and conferences. Rallies, peacewalks, and demonstrations are particularly effective when large groups of people remain standing mutely and stolidly still.

49. Renouncing special honors from the government which conferred them conveys, through self-sacrifice, a pointed message of repugnance to that government's policies. Such renunciations may include medals, honorary offices, titles of honor, and resignations from prestigious societies closely linked to the offending agency.

50. Turning one's back in silence is a means of showing disapproval towards politicians or officials who publicly represent a destructive principle.

*   *   *

The foregoing inventory contains, as we said earlier, the symbolic actions of protest and persuasion. As part of a citizen game plan to influence political decisions, these actions should fit midway between the confidence building strategies of conflict resolution and problem-solving in the next chapter, and the powerful deterrents of political noncooperation detailed in Appendix IX.

These three approaches to influencing government behavior — conflict resolution, symbolic actions, and political noncooperation — are entirely different, and it is important to keep them separate in the mind and to employ the most effective logical order when bringing them into play:

1) Friendly constructive negotiation should always be attempted first. This method presupposes that both sides have something to gain and something to lose from negotiation. If the government finds peace concerns irrelevant to its operations, then the citizens' next strategy is to proceed to

2) symbolic actions of protest and persuasion. These are reasonable tools for people to use to demonstrate to their governments the *unity of public concern* over the threat of nuclear war. Symbolic actions are a public opinion substitute for the current lack of representation of the nuclear arms issue at the polls. If this public unity is heard and respected, the government will agree to meet the peaceful coalitions at the negotiating table and there proceed to build workable solutions. If the government chooses *not* to listen, then the peace movement has little option but to resort to

3) the powerful methods of political noncooperation listed in Appendix IX. These are accompanied by an analysis of the nature and source of political power. Their use is only indicated when the party in power cannot be brought via other means to an awareness of the relevance of the issue at hand. Once the issue is perceived as relevant, it is possible to go back to square one, the negotiating table, and to build mutual solutions to commonly perceived problems.

Let us go now to that table, and to the methods that work best for both sides.

CHAPTER 12

NEGOTIATING FOR PEACE:
Winning For All

The purpose of this chapter is to help people at all levels of society to solve, by principled negotiation, the common human conflicts that ultimately lead to war. The techniques included here will apply to all conflicts in which the two sides have both shared and opposed interests, whether they be of a domestic, business, labor or political nature. We shall see how newly-emerging approaches to conflict resolution may change the whole emotional climate of problem-solving between parties who are caught in adversarial positions.

These new approaches are changing the negotiating climate from one of fear, mistrust, and foreboding to one of expectation for a solid, mutually acceptable outcome. As our cultural familiarity with these techniques grows and spreads, the time, energy, and unpleasantness that has been squandered in primitive dispute behaviors will be transformed into productive and fruitful negotiations. The big question is, will this embryonic alternative to raw dispute mature in time to avert a nuclear disaster?

The Primitive Nature of Raw Dispute

Imagine two big dogs, both eying the same bone, circling around it together, growling, hackles raised — and then the fur begins to fly. Or imagine two small children in a tug of war over the last candy cane on the Christmas tree. Tugs turn to shrieks, then to pushes and slaps. In both cases the struggle is simple: "*I* want this! You threaten my having it. I will *fight* you to get it."

With dogs and children it is easy to see how primitive and survival-based this ancient behavior is. But with adults, meeting together over varnished mahogany tables in business suits, we are not as apt to recognize what is less transparently the very same behavior. The fact is, that most people uneducated in the art of negotiation will enter a meeting wanting what they want and sensing that they are on a collision course with the other party. They arrive scared; they assume it will be a thinly masked push-pull conflict of raw interests, and that after much haggling, posturing, criticism, and humiliation, the more powerful or wily of the two sides will emerge victorious.

Both sides therefore arrive at the meeting prepared, having made firm decisions regarding their bottom lines, and having contrived aggressive positions which will allow them room to "bargain".

Party A says to himself, "I will accept a 7% raise over two years, but I will begin by demanding 9%." Party B calculates, "I am willing to raise his salary 4% but will start by declaring the company cannot afford more than 2%."

Thus they begin, too far away from their actual objectives, and too far apart to have their concerns taken seriously by the other side. The less they feel heard, the more strenuously they repeat themselves; and the more entrenched their positions become, the more emotional their attacks and accusations. Finally the whole focus of interest is the fight itself, with the original issue lost in the battle to save face. They break off and retreat to recuperate, like the two dogs.

Is Conflict Inevitable?

There is the story about the two men in the library, sharing a table by the window. First one gets up to open the window, then the other closes it. This is repeated several times; voices are raised. In comes the librarian to investigate the fuss. Mr. A wants the window open; Mr. B wants it shut. She asks A: "Why do you want the window open?" "To get some fresh air!" She turns to B: "Why do you want the window closed?" "Because the draft bothers my arthritis." The librarian thinks a moment, then walks to a room down the hall, and opens a window wide.

This story illustrates the difference between *positions* and *interests*. "Open" and "shut" were the conflicting positions the men took towards the window. They had no idea of what each other's underlying interest was because they stopped short of inquiring. Instead, distracted by the disharmony of their positions, each "locked into" his own. It was only when a third party intervened that it became possible to reconcile their interests by introducing a completely new "position" that each could accept.

This story demonstrates what a blind alley it is to identify one's interests with a single position. Interests are real and legitimate needs and requirements, whereas a position is simply one perceived method of securing an interest. And though opposing positions may be in conflict, the underlying interests may not. This confusion between interests and positions is thus one major source of avoidable dispute.

A second source of unnecessary conflict is the tendency to confuse a problem with the people who share in it. Mr. A and Mr. B, having become involved in a conflict of wills over their original positions, ended up in a shouting match to preserve their self-esteem. The problem itself, which concerned their interests, never came to light until it was examined on its own merits by someone whose ego and position were not at stake.

Conflicts, then, are not always inevitable. They often result from hasty assumptions, which in turn are based on a) confusion between legitimate interests and unimaginative positions, and b) confusions between other legitimate players in life and the problems we share with them."

Can We Avoid Conflict Systematically?
Gandhi was convinced that all disputes were the result of con-

flicting narrow perspectives on a common truth. In any given conflict, he said, both sides are handicapped by having a better view of their own truth than the truth of their opponent. Neither person has much initial interest in what is true for the other, yet that other separate reality and the perspective it entails is undeniably part of the overall picture. As long as they mutually deny one another's legitimacy, their perspectives remain too narrow to surmount the difficulty between them. While denial persists, they waste time, energy, and hard feelings in futile efforts to resist the larger truth that encompasses both positions.

To bring people mutually into focus over problems, Gandhi developed a procedure called *"satyagraha"*, which redirected the focus of the fight from persons to principles. This term literally translates into "grasping onto principles", or "truth-force".

In practice, this process involves looking for the truthful aspects of each side's position, then searching for a resolution broad enough to accommodate both of them, and holding fast to that.

The search for truth begins by identifying the elements within each perspective that are legitimate from both points of view. Each side enumerates all its points, and then both conduct a point-by-point inspection of each list.

Gandhi saw this inspection as a mutual and creative struggle to distinguish moral and principled goals from self-serving and destructive ones. In general, true or moral goals were those which affirmed life and harmony, while destructive goals were those which, in the service of power and pride, eroded human dignity.

Underlying all of Gandhi's beliefs was a deep love for the human being, and a corresponding respect for his dignity. To him, no dispute was ever completely settled until a solution was reached that took the truth of both parties equally into account. Failure to reach such a solution implied that either one of the sides had committed a violence towards the other by failing to see his truth, or that the other side had not held sufficiently fast to what was true for him. When violent solutions are imposed by stronger parties upon weaker ones, there is a perceived loss in dignity on the side of the weaker, and though overtly settled, inwardly the conflict continues to brew until dignity is restored.

Gandhi saw truth as a continuously unfolding phenomenon. The search never ended, for it involved an ongoing process of broadening one's perspective through interactions with others. *Satyagraha* was more of a dynamic in itself than a conclusion to be reached. It was a process of constant change, both inwardly in the self, and outwardly in society. It was a way of living in which the end *was* the means, and the means *were* the end. This "means-end", therefore, was the continuing process by which one lived — a principled search for the discovery of the largest perspective possible on all human interactions.

*   *   *

Let us return now to the problem at hand, the arms race. These weapons are the greatest affront to dignity and love that has ever been contrived. They are the vicious offspring of fear and mistrust, and they reduce the stature, confidence, and security of all who perceive their existence.

The only force on earth powerful and determined enough to eliminate these weapons is the "truth-force" of *satyagraha*, which is fired by love. It is to the intelligent application of this force that we shall now turn.

As individual citizens in the West we must begin by addressing our own relationships. How "clean" are they? How free of coercion, pride, and the need to control? How much effort do we give to the struggle of earning higher perspectives? And earn them we do. It is only our subjective "little i" nature that is automatic; any escape from this nature is a reprogramming which takes struggle and determination.

So the first step for concerned citizens in the peace movement is to take critical stock of their own lives to see how qualified they are to preach peace to their governments. For example, how much dignity and self-respect do we have for ourselves, and how much do we reserve for others? One thing is certain: it is not possible to allow even one other person to feel truly good about himself, truly loved, unless one knows what it is to feel truly good in oneself. And this involves seeing in oneself the whole uncanny miracle of the complete human being, with all his physical, spiritual and creative capacities. It means being able to love oneself in one's unique relationship to all of life, and then to accord that love to all others.

"All others" includes the fearful yet powerful representatives of nuclear policy.

What is required to change things is a great hierarchy in the *satyagraha* process, based at its foundation on individuals working together to make other people conscious of what they are losing through their submission to nuclear weapons.

All organized affinity groups — athletes, unions, women, churches, minorities, gays, professional associations, peace groups, etc. — are in a position to bring the spirit of *satyagraha* to bear, both within their own organizations and beyond them, and particularly to within their governments.

In Chapter 11 we looked at the nonviolent methods of resisting nuclear oppression. Now we must educate one another in the techniques which will build an alternative. As one Soviet historian has said, "The real issue today is not one of finding ways to improve and refine the methods of using force, but of excluding the use and threat of force from international relations."[1]

Where do we begin then?

Suppose you belong to a peace group called "Educators for Nuclear Disarmament" (END). You have finally managed, after weeks of waiting, to arrange a two-hour appointment with the City Council to discuss the possibility of making your city a nuclear-free zone. You know that the Mayor is a staunch supporter

152

of the federal administration, and that the city is home to a large number of defense contractors.

To give some structure to your preparation for the meeting, it might be useful to examine the negotiation model below:

Consider the following:

YOU

1. What do we need from the negotiation? Why?
2. What is our best alternative if we cannot come to an agreement?
3. What is our worst consequence if we cannot come to an agreement?
4. How important is the relationship to us?
5. What do we know about them, and what do we need to know?
6. Which areas do we agree upon?

THE OTHER PARTY

7. What do they need from the negotiation? Why?
8. What is their best alternative if we cannot come to an agreement?
9. What is the worst consequence for them if we cannot reach an agreement?
10. How important is the relationship to them?
11. Who else might be involved?

THE ISSUES

12. What information related to the issues do we need?
13. What information do the two parties need before they can make a decision?

THE APPROACH

14. What would be the best time and location for the first meeting?
15. What is our best opening approach?
16. What is their opening approach likely to be?

You sense as you look over the model that the City Council,

though vaguely in agreement that nuclear weapons are nasty things, has a much more immediate concern with the revenue generated locally by the defense plants. The City has no particular stake in its relationship with END however, and therefore needs nothing from the relationship with your group.

This is borne out by the opening remarks of the Mayor, whose opinion you politely solicit. He states emphatically that nuclear-free zones are bad for business and disrupt national security.

The disparity emerging here is not between positions and interests, but between the priorities given to interests, and what often determines priorities is the depth of imagination given to options.

Your task in this negotiation is first to convince Council that *we*, all citizens of the city, face a very serious threat: a) from the explosion of any nuclear weapon, accidental or otherwise, which would be many thousands of times more devastating than the Chernobyl disaster,[2] and b) from the fact that in the event of war, this city would be a logical target.

You might bring the devastating effects of nuclear explosions closer to mind by presenting highly specific slides of post-war Hiroshima and its victims. To view the slides you might ask everyone to sit along one side of the table, facing the problem on the screen together.

Following the slides, with everyone still seated on one side of the table, and with concern over vaguely nasty nuclear weapons elevated to a new level of priority, you might acknowledge the City's problem in being economically dependent upon the defense industry. Then you might invite both the Council and the teachers to paticipate in a short brainstorming session to create incentives that would encourage the city's defense plants to convert from military to non-military production.

In brainstorming, you first invite everyone to relax: have a cup of coffee and take off their jackets and ties, for example. Then you define the problem: "Our city is a probable nuclear target because it is a known center for the production of nuclear weapons parts." Then you invite people to participate in a rapid, free-associating flow of possible solutions to the problem. You emphasize the ground rule that there must be absolutely no criticism of the ideas that emerge, because people cannot open up to spontaneous creativity if they feel vulnerable to censure.

Many ideas, some quite wild, get tossed around in brainstorming. Perhaps someone comes up with the suggestion that a tax break be given to any plants that will convert from military production to human service products — for example, from biological warfare chemicals to life-giving vaccines. Someone else knows of a foundation that gives grants for vaccine research. Another person suggests that the City could beautify the lands and the highways adjacent to the plants which would be willing to convert. This move would raise the company's property values and the prestige of its surroundings; it would also stimulate summer employment for the college students.

Suddenly there is excitement in the room as it dawns on the group what has happened. Two groups have become one, with a new and creative perspective on a common problem. Common ground has emerged from separate interests.

The Mayor announces his intention to call a meeting in two weeks' time with the managers of the three major plants, and he promptly invites his financial officer and two members of END.

The example above employs nine of the many techniques of principled negotiation which are presented in the splendid little book "Getting to YES"[3] by Fisher and Ury. All of these techniques demonstrate that principled negotiation is a far more unifying approach to problem-solving than is the customary positional bargaining.

The techniques you used above, in the order that they appeared, are recapped below:

1) Ask the other side questions. Find out what they really think, for their thinking often *is* the problem.

2) Let the other side blow off steam if he needs to, and listen quietly and respectfully while the energy winds down. Do not engage in an argument while emotions are being discharged. The sooner the other side feels heard and respected, the sooner it will be possible to progress beyond positions to the merits of the problem.

3) When people find fault and assess blame ("nuclear-free zones are bad for business and disrupt national security"), it is usually because they are entangling people (as in the peace movement) with problems. Avoid confusing people with problems, particularly if the other side is falling into this trap already.

Principled negotiation separates the people from the positions they are in. It is hard on the merits of the positions, but soft on the people themselves. It does not employ tricks or postures to gain advantage, nor does it otherwise violate the trust it seeks to encourage between people.

4) Identify basic shared interests that will lead to common ground. Avoiding the possibility of a local Hiroshima is about as basic as things can be.

5) Be specific; bring your interests to life for the other side so that he can credit the sincerity of your concerns. Photographs are highly specific.

6) Present the substance of the problem as one that requires joint attention to solve, and refer to objective criteria (such as statistics about Hiroshima) to define and analyze the problem.

7) It helps to seat people on opposing sides of an issue along the same side of a room, facing the common problem together. This stresses the unity of the group in seeking a truthful solution, with attention focused on the problem itself and not on one another.

8) Acknowledge the interests of the other side; paraphrase them to show that you have heard and understood them. Then return to your common ground as a starting place in the search for options that will satisfy both sides.

9) Create as many options as possible to avoid "digging in" to opposing positions.

Brainstorming is a mutual and creative approach to unearthing the group unconscious and building superb ideas. It may be used within your group before the meeting, or, if the atmosphere is relaxed, by the two parties together.

The strategies illustrated above are but a very few of the immensely useful suggestions contained in "Getting to YES". Simple and practical, it is bound to improve harmony in relationships for all who read it. A good summary paragraph from this book reads:

> "In contrast to positional bargaining, the principled negotiation method of focusing on basic interests, mutually satisfying options, and fair standards typically results in a wise agreement. The method permits you to reach a gradual consensus on a joint decision *efficiently* without all the transactional costs of digging in to positions only to have to dig yourself out of them. And separating the people from the problem allows you to deal directly and empathetically with the other negotiator as a human being, thus making possible an *amicable* agreement."[4]

*　　*　　*

It is now time to consider what we might anticipate from the application of *satyagraha* or principled negotiation techniques to talks between the Soviet Union and the West. But before we examine the issues involved, we should ask ourselves the question from the model, "What do we know about them, and what do we need to know?"

Perhaps the most striking thing about educated and even liberal spokesmen for the Soviet Union is their perception of the capitalist system. Living and breathing in it as we do, it is really quite mind-stretching to stand outside of our familiar culture and see it through Soviet eyes.

Very briefly, then, Soviet political philosophy, based upon the tenets of Marx and Engels, finds injustice in an economy which, driven by the profit motive, subordinates a working class to an ownership class in a relationship which is seen as fundamentally exploitative. Because capitalism is left to run by its profit dynamic, it is considered to be rudderless, full of contradictions and opposing interests, and basically violent and dangerous.

The Soviets perceive the West as out of control, with the interests of the common man sacrificed to the vested interests of a military-industrial ruling class. Reading the speeches of Mikhail Gorbachev,[5,6] or the careful formulations of Professor Georgi Arbatov,[7] one finds sincerity and conviction in their concerns over the power and unpredictability of capitalism.

There is no question in their minds at all as to who instigated the nuclear arms race, and indeed it is difficult to dispute their points. The weapons, extraordinarily difficult to make, were created by Western determination, and for years America maintained a comfortable lead in their development. When the Soviet Union caught up, however, the United States, in what the Soviets regard as a desperate measure to regain their lost lead, declared its willingness to resort to first use offensives and to engage in limited nuclear war. Now, they say, unable to tolerate the stabilizing equality of deterrence, the U.S. is committing billions of dollars to extend the race to space, a move which is also bolstering its sagging, debt-ridden economy.

Soviet critics say capitalism lacks positive aims and orientations for the working class, which creates problems of unemployment, soaring health care costs, and the neglect of the poor and the elderly. Also they perceive that the real intent of United States policy in "protecting the free world" is not so much to bring minimal standards of food and health care to developing countries as it is to serve the market and labor needs of a flagging capitalism.

So much for how we are perceived. Now let us turn to current developments within the Soviet Union. In this regard, it is worth reading Gorbachev's speeches to the CPSU Central Committee, because they contain good objective analysis of Soviet political shortcomings, while offering imaginative reforms for the coming years. If one is inclined to dismiss him as a clever politician, then let the record speak for itself.

March 11, 1987 marked the second anniversary of Gorbachev's ascent to leadership. Since April, 1985, the following steps[8] have been taken:

1985

March	Gorbachev chosen General Secretary of Communist Party.
April	Major economic reforms promised.
	Campaign against state corruption announced.
May	Crackdown on the consumption of liquor begins.
	More land is made available for private farming.
July	Financial incentives introduced for scientists and engineers.
August	*Moratorium on nuclear testing begins.*
October	Major program to increase supply of consumer goods begins.
	Plan to cut superpower weapons by 50% proposed.

1986

January	*Plan to eliminate all nuclear weapons by year 2000 proposed.*
February	Anatoly Shcharansky released from prison and allowed to leave for Israel.
	Key speech[5] criticizes Soviet Union as too centralized; introduces idea of "supply and demand" for consumer goods.
March	Soviet journalists urged to stop writing "drivel" and report the facts.
	Beatles' records go on sale.
April	Financial incentives offered to grain farmers, based on output.
	Large-scale troops cuts in Eastern Europe proposed.
June	Soviet theatre encouraged to portray real life.

July   *On-site verification of nuclear weapons proposed.*
              Officials at Chernobyl nuclear plant cited as negligent in
              reactor accident.
August   Works by banned Soviet writer Boris Pasternak and Rus-
              sian-born Vladimir Nabokov to be published.
              Moscow applies to join GATT, the General Agreement
              on Tariffs and Trade.
              Principle of aerial inspection of military exercises ac-
              cepted, in anticipation of Stockholm talks.
October   *8,000 Soviet soldiers withdrawn from Afghanistan.*
              Soviet dissident Yuri Orlov released from prison and al-
              lowed to emigrate.
November   New labor law allows limited free enterprise and sala-
              ries according to performance.
December   Physicist Andrei Sakharov freed from internal exile and
              allowed to speak freely.
              "Is it Easy to be Young", domestic film critical of Soviet
              war in Afghanistan, released.

                                    1987

January   Proposal of secret ballots and multiple candidates in
              elections.
              Joint corporate ventures with Western countries encour-
              aged with tax breaks.
              Several expatriate artists, such as Mikhail Baryshnikov,
              invited to Soviet Union to perform freely.
              Jamming of BBC's Russian broadcasts stopped.
              Senior KGB official dismissed for interfering with re-
              porter who exposed corruption by Government official.
February   Crime of criticizing the State to be dropped.
              Pravda begins publishing letters to the editors critical of
              the Communist Party.
              Three hundred dissidents released.
              Economic reform law published, introducing role for
              profits.
              On-site inspection of chemical weapons proposed.
              Elimination of medium-range nuclear missiles in Eu-
              rope proposed.
              18-month moratorium on nuclear weapons testing
              abandoned after first U.S. blast of 1987, in January.

It is difficult to know what more Mr. Gorbachev could do, unilaterally, to demonstrate his willingness to meet Mr. Reagan halfway. During the time period above, Mr. Reagan announced (May 1986) that he would no longer be bound by SALT II, and on Thanksgiving Eve, against the wishes of both Congress and his allies, he scrapped the SALT II limits by deploying the 131st strategic bomber equipped with Cruise Missiles. Meanwhile, during the 18-month Soviet moratorium on nuclear testing, the U.S. exploded at least 22 bombs, 12 of which exceeded the 20-kiloton limit set by the 1974 Threshold Test Ban Treaty, which was signed by both countries but is still not ratified.

However things may have been in the past between East and West, the facts listed above are clear and well-documented. As the Soviet Union opens up, we begin to see "the enemy" more as he sees himself. We find with increasing information that his intentions are peaceful, though he is wary of ours. And is that not precisely how we feel ourselves?

*   *   *

When Western leaders join their Eastern counterparts at the Summit bargaining table, they must be particularly careful to understand the structure of their own assumptions about the Soviets. We analyzed such assumptions in Chapter 9, in the chart called "The Circle of Enmity", which shows the influence of fear upon reality.

Our leaders must become as clear as possible about what actual Soviet intentions *are*. This means *listening* — listening with everything we've got to the totality of Soviet interests.

Active listening is a profoundly valuable gift to someone who is seriously speaking his mind, yet it costs nothing at all to give. When a person in difficulty senses that his interests are being truly heard, he is validated by the quiet, receptive attention that is focused upon him, and he opens up and works his thinking into view — into his own view and into the view of the other.

Listening is a silent generosity which helps other people to see and know and accept themselves as they explore the depths that this unresisting validation allows to surface in them.

Carl Rogers refers to this art of creative listening as "empathic listening". In his words, "Empathy dissolves alienation",[9] and "Empathy is clearly related to positive outcome."[10] This is so because empathy provides the confidence for discovering previously unknown elements in the self. This new knowledge leads to a change in self-concept, and soon behavior begins to fall into line with the freshly perceived self.

We asked in Chapter 9: "Does our picture of the enemy have the power to influence its object?" The answer is "yes". Yes, it can make the enemy wary, guarded, and mistrustful, or yes, it can make him open, trusting, and secure. It is all in how we hear him, how we react to his reality. How we hear him depends upon our own capacity for love, and how we react depends upon whether we choose to build *satyagraha* with him or not.

This choice reveals our fundamental orientation towards the humanity of other people. Let us now examine, in the light of an affirmative choice, what broad steps might be taken to forge common interests with the Soviet Union.

*   *   *

The most powerful human interests are the basic human needs, and these are universal: security; economic well-being; a sense of belonging and recognition; and control over one's life.

Different political systems address these needs in a variety of different ways. This is a fact *secondary* to the interests themselves. Does the fact of different systems justify structuring the planet into a divided hierarchy dependent upon the motives of two superpowers who are artificially stimulating the world economy with weapons of mass destruction? Does this structure really meet the world's needs for security and economic well-being?

Below is a list of problems which are undermining human well-being in the world today:

Terrorism	Suicide
Vast national debts	Religious conflicts
Social unrest	Divorce
Alcohol and drug abuse	Hunger
	Disease
Nuclear weapons	Police brutality
Crime and violence	Trade disputes
International aggression	Flashpoints of military danger

Surely our foremost interests lie in solving these common dilemmas of modern civilization. Yet when the superpowers meet at the bargaining table, as at Reykjavik (October 1986), they end up in focused disagreement on perhaps *one* aspect of *one* of the above concerns: whether to weaken the AMB Treaty of 1972 with a weapons race in outer space, or whether to stick to the Treaty and scuttle Star Wars. (They finished, incidentally, in an exact reversal of the positions they took over antiballistic missiles in the 1968-1970 period.)

How does this high-level obsession with "security within conflict" advance our basic human needs? The answer is that there can no longer be security *of any kind* on this earth until we recognize our most primary interest as the goal of international cooperation.

Real cooperation already does take place at lower levels, particularly in science and medicine. It was through working together as cardiologists that Drs. Yevgeni Chazov and Bernard Lown conceived the idea of forming International Physicians for the Prevention of Nuclear War, which won the Nobel Peace Prize in 1985. (Dr. Chazov has recently been appointed Minister of Health for the Soviet Union.)

It is at the *Summit* talks that the focus must switch from bargaining over weapons to negotiating for the interests of people. This means *dropping* Star Wars and nuclear tests (the latter being the cornerstone for the arms race and of no real benefit to ordinary people), and sitting down to discuss the common interests of our societies.

The following agenda could be used as a model for Summit negotiation. The process of *satyagraha* can begin anywhere, so either side could suggest this format for the talks:

Steps in Negotiation	Agenda
I. Identify the needs of both sides	1. Both superpower negotiators would indicate in their opening speeches the particular internal social and economic problems they would address within their own country if the military budget were to be reduced by 50%.
II. List common goals	2. The sides would together form a list of internal problems that both had opted to solve. These might include poverty, farm productivity, drug and alcohol addiction, and AIDS.
III. Take joint action	3. Both sides would sign an agreement to appoint top people to steering committees to explore ways of solving these problems.
IV. Identify further concerns	4. Both leaders would then identify the priority international problems that each would address after the reduction in military spending.
V. List common needs, etc.	5. Again a common list would be drawn up, expert groups assigned to working committees, and arrangements made for future meetings.

Negotiating for Peace

At the close of the Summit, having worked together for good and invigorating ends, and having put fear and the weapons of fear in their proper place on the agenda (last), the problem of intricately bargaining them out of our lives would suddenly seem absurd.

These weapons are an obsession of the mind, and they cannot be bargained away. The only way out is to *forget* them: dismantle them. They are instruments of fear and oppression, and as such they have no place in *satyagraha,* no connection to the love or truth between humans. These weapons are ultimately fear itself, and we must put *that* away or die.

CHAPTER 13

INDIVIDUAL OPPORTUNITIES:
"What Can I Do?"

Let us begin this final chapter by recapping a little.

The nuclear weapons powers are in the grip of irrational forces which are driving the arms race towards the specter of nuclear war and nuclear winter. The existing political systems do not seem adequate to control this lemming-like drive towards planetary oblivion.

Our present peril is without parallel in history, and a new political force, also without parallel, is needed to control it. What is needed now is a transnational movement of "planetary citizens", whose first commitment is the abolition of the warfare system. These citizens must work efficiently and effectively to promote a widespread change in attitudes. They must organize themselves into nonviolent action groups, and through education and publicity build a momentum of citizen involvement that culminates in a massive interventionist democracy (MID). This massive interventionist democracy should withdraw its support for the warfare system, and build in its place the East-West networks that will foster creative solutions.

People traditionally active in the nuclear disarmament movement should now begin to view themselves as planetary citizens whose first loyalty is towards continued life on earth. Their goal should be not simply the removal of the weapons themselves, but the unification of mankind against the violence he builds into the weapons. The weapons cannot disappear until the problem is traced to its source *within* man.

166

Individual Opportunities

This goal of unity must be pursued along three tracks. The first is to overcome the political barriers to peace with the Soviets by developing a network of personal communication with them at the individual level. The second is to reduce the military budgets of Western nuclear countries by widespread tax refusal. The third is to recruit a citizen majority that will press Western governments to earnestly negotiate for peace.

* * *

Bridges of Communication to the Soviet Peoples

Viewed one way, the crux of the nuclear danger is very simple. The Soviet and American nations face each other, like two huge pyramids, with only the men on top (who are yelling at each other) in communication. (See Diagram 6.)

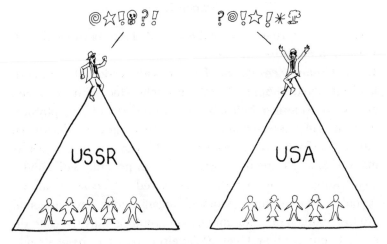

Diagram 6.

These men can only get away with their yelling and their nuclear roulette game if the vast number of people below seldom talk to one another. What is needed is an extensive bridgework of personal communication between the people who populate these pyramids. (See Diagram 7.) The broader the base of personal relationships between the two cultures, the less credibility the posturings at the top will have.

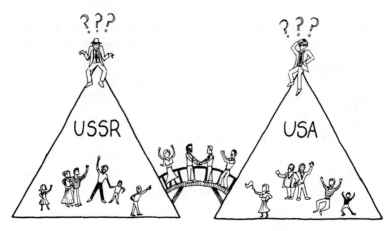

Diagram 7.

Let us now turn to some of the ways that interpersonal Soviet-Western friendships may begin:

1. *The Ground Zero Pairing Project,* with headquarters in Portland, Oregon (see Appendix III) encourages the pairing of Soviet and North American cities, based on similarity of size, physical environment, and economic base. The Project is educational rather than political in character, and its aim is to connect as many U.S. and Canadian communities as possible with similar communities in the USSR. This paired city concept allows schools, religious groups, women's organizations, environmental groups, sportsmen, entertainers, and youth groups to relate directly to one another. Over 1000 pairing packages have already been sent from American and Canadian cities to cities in the Soviet Union, and there have been group visits between members of the paired communities. The Project has been sensibly and realistically organized and has good educational materials.

Pairing usually begins with the exchanging of community portraits. These include greetings and messages from mayors, city councils, and residents; a copy of a local newspaper; photographs of the area; and perhaps some children's art. For those seeking to identify a suitable Russian city, the Great Soviet Encyclopedia is available in most college libraries.

2. *The Pen-twin Concept* was originated by Professor Ferenc Mezei, Hungarian Academy of Sciences, and Professors Luis Sobrino and Geoffrey Hoffman of the University of British Columbia in Vancouver. It outlines a program for linking up the citizens of East and West on a one-to-one letter-writing basis. These professors envision millions of Western "diplomats" working in parallel with millions of Eastern "diplomats", who, in times of deepening tensions, might step up their correspondence to dispel the tension, rather than breaking off contact and retreating into silence, as governments often do.

The idea is to reduce the possibility of nuclear war through a simple action that anyone can do, which is to form a permanent correspondence with a Soviet citizen of similar age and occupation. In becoming a pen-twin, one undertakes to write to his or her pen-twin once a year (preferably a simple, friendly, unpolitical letter), and to encourage friends and associates to seek out a pen-twin as well.

Letters from the West would usually be written in English, with the onus of interpretation upon one's Soviet "twin". The Soviets would reply in Russian, though some correspondence may be conducted entirely in English, as there are more people *teaching* English in Russia than there are people in the United States *studying* Russian. Esperanto, which will be discussed later, is available as a common language for written communication.

As confidence builds up between the pen-twins, they may wish to explain to one another that they do not personally support their government's activities in Nicaragua, for example, or Afghanistan. In this way frozen stereotypes of East and West as faceless, mindless supporters of politically incompatible regimes might begin to thaw out in the popular consciousness of both sides. Again it is a matter of displacing the wariness and distrust at the top with openness and good will below. As a spirit of friendliness ripples and grows, the stockpiles of nuclear weapons will lose support and relevance in the common mind.

Pentwin Albums explaining the concept in greater detail are available for $5.00 from the University of British Columbia Bookstore, 6200 University Boulevard, Vancouver, B.C., Canada, V6T 1Y5, telephone (604) 228-4741.

What is the best way to contact a pen-twin? There are several possibilities: a) contact the USSR-USA Society, House of Friendship With Peoples of Foreign Countries, 14 Kalinin Prospect, Moscow, USSR, 103009; b) write to an Eastern European magazine which carries a penpal column, such as *World Youth*, 1389 Budapest, P.O.B. 147, Hungary; c) contact a penpal agency within your own country; and d) consult a public library for directories of Soviet universities, libraries, hospitals or schools, and write to ask whether any individual at that address might wish to strike up a correspondence with you. The Soviet central agencies for the various groups shown in Appendix IV might also be helpful in recruiting individuals who would like to work for peace through a pen-twin network.

It is important to remember that the Russian mails are slow (allow 4-8 weeks for delivery), and that there are close restrictions on what may enter the country by mail. (The Ground Zero Pairing Project will supply current and detailed information on these restrictions.)

If the idea of a penfriend network were to catch on in schools, children might encourage their parents to take it up. One teacher asked her students to draw pictures of missiles and tanks being converted to peaceful and life-giving activities. The children loved it because it involved technology. Through these positive actions, children and adolescents allay some of the helplessness they feel from the threat of nuclear war.

Individual Opportunities

This concept of pen-twinning has great potential to break down false stereotypes and to reverse the process of dehumanization that traditionally leads to war. It cannot work, though, unless each person takes his small but essential share in the initiative, a tiny step to begin with, but one that could blossom into friendship, travel, and greatly expanded horizons.

3. *Esperanto* was developed in the 1880's as a language of international communication by Dr. L.L. Zamenhof. It is a very simple language, built upon 15,000 of the most internationally used word roots, and has a regular system of prefixes and suffixes which promote the easy formation of words. The World Esperanto Organization has members in over 100 countries, and holds more than 100 conferences each year in Esperanto, without using translation or interpreters. There is much original and translated literature in Esperanto, including works of fiction, non-fiction, poetry, prose, and drama. It is used to publish over 100 regular magazines, and radio stations in some dozen countries broadcast in it.

Our world, with its 3000-4000 tongues, has language as one of its most significant barriers to global unification and peace. Each language has the personality and color of its regional background and cultural traditions. When a person drops his own language to speak the language of another, he is disadvantaged by having to communicate on less comfortable terms than the other — by having to relate, so to speak, through the cultural personality of the other's language. People who speak Esperanto claim that because of its cultural neutrality, it delights the speakers with a completely new communication experience by immersing them in a clean, fresh, and open frame of mind. Above all, perhaps, it introduces language equality, and is therefore a promising channel for personal contact, both spoken and written, between East and West. For further information and addresses, see Appendix V.

4. *Video exchanges by satellite* offer exciting new possibilities as a stage for East-West communication and rapport. In late 1984,

for example, the Beyond War movement in Palo Alto, California featured a satellite video exchange between 3200 people in San Francisco and a smaller crowd in Moscow. This "Spacebridge", which has subsequently been televised, allowed the American and Soviet audiences the pleasure of waving to each other half a world away.

The Beyond War Award was presented by Spacebridge to the Five Continent Peace Initiative member nations (Mexico, Argentina, Sweden, Tanzania, Greece and India) in December 1985.

In March 1986, Soviet and American women aired common problems through a televised satellite hook-up, moderated by talk-show host Phil Donahue in the Needham Studio, and Soviet commentator Vladimir Pozner in Leningrad. This Citizens' Summit was televised widely in both countries.

Representatives from the Soviet and American governments have agreed to hold a series of satellite TV discussions in 1987 to air such issues as human rights and arms control before their two countries.

These are only the first steps in what could become a world-transforming medium. Groups of people everywhere could come face to face with one another, mirroring each other's humanity in the common realization that the world is indeed one home for all of us.

5. *Visits, and exchanges of children,* especially between influential American and Soviet citizens, are real life events which help to counterbalance the dry, stale images of communists and capitalists that exist in stereotype. After their own stereotype-breaking experience at the Geneva Summit, Reagan and Gorbachev planned the late 1986 exchange of 10 young Soviets with 10 young Americans, all of whom shared an interest in space exploration and astronomy.

Peace groups also plan exchanges for children. In August 1986, "Kids Meeting Kids Can Make a Difference" sent 10 American youths, aged 10 to 15, to meet 10 Soviet youngsters in Moscow.

They visited three Soviet cities and spent a week in a camp on the Black Sea. Then the Earthstewards Network set up an exchange in which 20 Soviet teenagers visited as many American teens in their homes for three weeks during the fall of 1986.

In Papua, New Guinea, when certain warring tribes make peace, they exchange a child. Growing up with each other's tribe, the two children keep in touch with their own people and thus ensure against future conflict.

Though in times of detente Western governments have developed official exchange programs with the Soviet Union in the fields of culture, education, sports, and entertainment, all too often these programs are canceled the moment the Soviets step out of line, as they did in Afghanistan. The cancellations arising over Afghanistan have recently been reversed to some extent, as witnessed by the August 1986 agreement between the United States and the Soviet Union on 13 new arts exchange programs. This agreement is expected to return the two countries to a level of cultural and educational exchange that they have not had since the *detente* years. In November 1986, Canada dropped the sanctions it imposed on Russia over Afghanistan, with External Affairs Minister Joe Clark commenting that "Sanctions do not work . . . It makes more sense to influence their behaviour by our contacts with them."

It is precisely when tensions are escalating that we must *rely* on these precious cultural ties, not sever them. It is therefore essential that as many exchange programs as possible develop within the private sector — between universities, schools, professional organizations, environmental groups, performers, sportsmen, and entertainers.

The Soviets have been hosting a number of large international peace campaigns during the last year or two. In May 1986, 150 scholars from 47 countries, including three from Canada, joined 500 Soviet experts in Moscow at the Second National Conference of Soviet Scientists on Peace and the Prevention of War.

Again in Moscow, 74 countries and thousands of athletes, coaches and officials took part in the July 1986 Goodwill Games, which were organized by the Olympic committees and scheduled to be alternately hosted by the USSR and the United States every four years, with Game Two to be held in Detroit in 1990.

Gregory Peck, Yoko Ono, and Graham Greene were among 1000 cultural, scientific and political figures from 80 countries who participated in a Moscow forum on peace and nuclear arms in February 1987. Dr. Mary-Wynne Ashford, Vice-President of Canadian Physicians for the Prevention of Nuclear War, attended this forum and was delighted to find Soviet society in a state of dynamic change, with open discussion and even criticism of Soviet policies in Afghanistan.

Anyone who can afford to go — lone travellers, couples, families, women's organizations, or members of local peace groups — contributes to the universally growing awareness that the two cultures are, more than anything else, living groups of real people who share in the fullness of human life.

Controlling Western Military Budgets

With regard to military spending, nuclear democracies have been given a virtually blank cheque. After all, we are told, isn't the whole country, aren't all other programs placed in jeopardy, if "they" get ahead of "us"? The big advocates of military spending are making too much money, and are too frightened by their lack of faith in human nature to self-restrain their own "defense" budgets. It is not the nature of the beast to cut itself in size.

It is, therefore, up to the rest of us — up to those who *write* their cheques — to slow these funds down at source. But once again, to even consider this, we must get out of the habit of feeling like children in relation to "the authorities". They are hired to do our bidding, and if, for example, in town hall meetings across the land there emerged a popular will to eliminate the nuclear war system of preserving peace, then we should *mean business* by that, and refuse to pay for the weapons. After all, we are willing to die for democracy, so why not *use* it?

If any person does not wish to comply with his elected government's *request* that he pay taxes for supplying weapons of mass destruction, there is no earthly reason why he should do so. Survival is our first premise, and if the arms race is folly, we are fools to support it, let alone *pay* for it!

Many courageous people have, over the years, been quietly doing just that — refusing to pay the military portion of their taxes — and the thinking goes as follows.

The principle of conscientious objection respects the dictates of individual conscience (whether on religious, moral, political, or philosophical grounds) to determine whether or not a person will participate in war. This principle has been applied to all possible levels of participation: to armed combat, to nonviolent military service, to civilian support of the war effort, and to paying taxes.

In American law, a person may object to war service on grounds of conscience provided that he objects to all war and not just to a particular war. This law does not, however, sanction the non-payment of military taxes.

The laws of society are always in flux, constantly evolving to meet our developing standards for the dignity and equality of human beings. Technology is also in flux, and nuclear weapons technology has extended the risks of combat from the armed forces to the whole civilian world. Participation in war has been redefined by these weapons: it is now a matter of paying taxes and waiting for annihilation. If the only way to participate in a war effort is to pay taxes, then the only way to withdraw from it is to refuse taxes. If it is illegal to refuse military taxes, however, then the constitutional right to object to killing no longer exists. This is a *key* point, and for each person who loathes the presence of these weapons, the law is out of step with a conscience. If conscience is to be true to itself it must act now to update

175

the law to the nuclear age, or otherwise risk the consequences.

If the right to withhold taxes for nuclear weapons is to gain sanction in law, then it must be differentiated from the crime of tax evasion. Here is where the peace tax concept comes in: this idea is a stroke of genius.

When income tax is *not* deducted at source (taken off by the employer and forwarded directly to the federal government), people may identify the portion of their income tax which is destined for military use (about 12-14%) and subtract it from their payment along with a letter of explanation. This letter might read as follows: "As a matter of conscience I cannot contribute to the financial support of nuclear weapons, and am therefore reluctantly withholding the military portion of my income tax. I do, however, appreciate the realities of international conflicts and am willing to direct the withheld percentage of my taxes into alternative means of conflict resolution. Should you wish to collect my conflict resolution dollars, you could establish a Peace Tax Office to research the causes of war. Its revenue could be used to relieve the hunger and economic disparities which give rise to international violence and instability.

"As no official peace tax agency yet exists in this country, I am sending, by today's mail, a cheque in the amount of (12-14% of my income tax) to our national citizens' peace tax fund. This is a private fund which is trying to fill the vacuum of peaceful solutions which exists through government default. Yours optimistically."

If you were to take the action described above, you would become a "peace truster". (Each letter of resistance from a peace truster is calculated to represent about 200 unexpressed opinions.) Peace trusters have organized themselves into national groups in 28 countries and hold international conferences. Addresses for some of the national organizations are listed in Appendix VI.

The peace tax movement began in the United States in 1971,

with thousands of activities going on among churches, local community groups, regional and state-wide groups, and national organizations. The Philadelphia Annual Meeting, for example, which is the oldest Quaker Meeting in America, has been refusing to forward the war taxes of its employees since 1979. When its members are taken to court, the Meeting pays their penalties.

Conscience Canada in Victoria, British Columbia offers a good model for running a peace tax fund. It publishes a lively and informative quarterly newsletter which provides international scope on matters of war and conscience. Each issue includes three pages of letters from concerned peace trusters to the Minister of Revenue Canada.

Among the uses to which peace tax funds are put is the payment of court costs and fines that result from government actions. The current U.S. situation is that though thousands of cases have gone through the courts, all to date have either been lost or denied access to the Supreme Court. But the movement is growing, and as more and more defense dollars are diverted to challenging military spending through the courts, the more crowded the courts become, and the closer the country gets to a constitutional resolution of the issue.

Massive Interventionist Democracy

The methods we have been looking at so far have had broad application to anyone in search of peaceful solutions. (There is a detailed summary of these and other methods in Appendix VII.) It is now time to touch upon the options available to people in specific occupations and walks of life.

We will look first at the physicians, to whom it occurred early that they should speak out loud and clear on the medical impossibility of coping with "the final epidemic".

The U.S. organization Physicians for Social Responsibility (PSR), and the International Physicians for the Prevention of Nuclear War (IPPNW) have been actively publicizing the medical consequences of nuclear war, and urging people to take preventive action before it is too late. The IPPNW Congress meets each year in May or June, with over 4000 delegates at Cologne in 1986 representing 160,000 physicians from 49 countries. In 1984 over one million physicians from 83 countries — about a quarter of the world's doctors — signed the International Physicians' Call for an End to the Nuclear Arms Race and presented it to this Congress.

The Soviet Government supports IPPNW and is hosting the 1987 Congress in Moscow. The Minister of Health for the Soviet Union is Dr. Yevgeni Chazov, co-founder of IPPNW with Dr. Bernard Lown of Harvard. Following the 1982 meeting, returning Soviet delegates addressed 100 million Soviet television viewers in an unedited, uncensored, and unrehearsed broadcast dealing with the medical aftermath of nuclear war. The Hippocratic Oath has been expanded, in a move endorsed by the Presidium, to commit Soviet physicians to work for the prevention of nuclear war. There are now over 20,000 doctors organized in the Soviet Union to prevent nuclear war by informing the people of its medical consequences.

In the United States, the American Medical Association and the American College of Physicians have adopted resolutions urging their members to recognize that there is no effective medical response to nuclear war, and recommending that they inform their colleagues, patients, and political representatives of its actual medical consequences and of prevention as its only cure.

Physicians for Social Responsibility, based in Boston, was formed in the 1960's and was reorganized in 1980. It is now functioning in over 150 chapters across the United States, has 23 chapters in Canada, and is developing courses for medical school curricula and educating the public through seminars and symposia. Its members have written and edited some excellent educational books.[1,2,3,4] PSR has emboldened other professions to take up the cause of social responsibility, and there are now a number of flourishing counterparts, including scientists, lawyers, educators, nurses, social workers, psychologists, engineers, businessmen, entertainers, artists, and others too numerous to mention.

The concerned physician is uniquely placed to advise his or her patients that most human health problems are dwarfed by the escalating threat of nuclear war, and that the only solution lies in prevention. This may be briefly presented at the end of the consultation, together with fact-sheets on the medical consequences and suggestions for citizen intervention.

On a lighter note, the dentist has a made in heaven opportunity to bend his patient's ear!

The teacher's voice is widely heard and influential. Many educators' groups are working to raise awareness of peace issues, to identify (usually drastic) shortcomings in the school curricula, and to develop strategies for cooperative problem-solving and nonviolent conflict resolution for the classroom.

Teachers should know that children in all countries are deeply concerned about the threat of nuclear war. Recent surveys of 12-18 year-olds in Canada, the USA, the USSR, Sweden, and Finland show that about one in four children claim to live for immediate gratification only, because the future is too uncertain to allow for marriage and family planning. Children need adults who will listen to these fears and who will show, by taking action themselves, that they do *not* accept annihilation as their fate, that they do *not* feel helpless in preventing nuclear war.

Children today need better tools with which to craft their fate. The stone-age model of the "tribe" or the "enemy" must give way to a new model of unity and inter-relatedness which will match the new terms of our survival. Education must therefore seek to impart:

1) the sense that human beings the world over are as real to themselves as we are; that each person is "me" to himself, and that this fundamental "me-ness" is the same in everyone;

2) the capacity to empathize with and care for the ways and feelings of other "me's";

3) the ability to value and practice sharing, cooperation, and nonviolent conflict resolution;

4) the capacity to give to other people, even at cost to oneself;

5) a vital appreciation for the global inter-relatedness of human well-being;

6) the willingness to be aware of major world problems in human welfare, the desire to see these solved, and the commitment and priority to address them;

7) the awareness of activities and channels which promote social change.

Children should therefore be taught about Third World problems, about problem-solving international institutions such as the United Nations, and about domestic democratic processes. In particular, the age-old fascination with war games, toys, and strategies should be channeled into peaceful competition. The instinct to test oneself against others can no longer be pursued through violence. As Martin Luther King Jr. put it, "The choice today is no longer between violence and non-violence. It is either non-violence or non-existence."

Most North Americans know very little about day to day life in the Soviet Union. Teaching must widen our experience of Russian nursery rhymes, fables, folklore, songs, customs, celebrations, sports, religion, family life, and agriculture, so that the emphasis is on common ground rather than upon the missile count.

Parents may form *Parents for Peace* and together urge schools and universities to officially include peace-building on the curriculum, and to place informative books and films on peace, justice, and militarism in their libraries. They may also promote the airing of unifying or "globalizing" films on local television.

Parents and teachers may attend workshops together to plan educational strategies. Remembrance Day activities, whole school peace days, and media events may be staged to promote global awareness. These activities may include songs such as "The Universal Soldier", debates, artwork competitions, student forums, and mock parliaments.

UNESCO sponsored the World Congress on Disarmament Education in Paris in 1980 and 1981. These were attended by the World Confederation of Organizations of the Teaching Profession (WCOTP), which represents some seven million teachers from 185 teacher organizations in 86 countries. In 1982 WCOTP urged governments to "adopt a policy of seeking ways to halt the arms race and bring about general, controlled, and phased disarmament".

Teachers everywhere who are concerned for the future safety and security of their children should keep in mind the United Nations Declaration of the Rights of the Child: "He shall be brought up in a spirit of understanding, tolerance, friendship among peoples, peace and universal brotherhood, and in full consciousness that his energy and talents should be devoted to the service of his fellow man."

Lawyers for Social Responsibility is an international, nonprofit organization of judges, lawyers, legal secretaries, law librarians, and others. The legal implications of restructuring the world for peace are vast and far-reaching. Domestically, the use of civil disobedience to promote disarmament initiatives is a fragile embryo in need of nurture and support. Concerned but uncertain people would take heart from the knowledge that there was an informed, committed, and available legal resource to shepherd them through the courts.

As the maw of global militarization gorges itself on the world's food and health dollars (world military spending exceeded $800 billion dollars in 1985), it also feeds people's energy and determination for peace. Sooner or later the principles of conscience in a world poised for oblivion will have to be tested constitutionally in the Supreme Court. It is ultimately a question of the status of our democracy — is it real or is it whitewash? The law schools and librarians and judges and justices will need to be humanly ready and professionally equipped to serve the country and the world on this most urgent and paramount of constitutional issues.

Another immense issue, and one which will need ultimately to be resolved through international law, is the growing feeling in favor of world government. In recent decades the speed of communications has produced a network of economic ties between countries which is far more persuasive than the divisions created by borders. Though the human community is behaving economically like one large interconnected body, the body lacks a head. Politically the parts of the body remain severed by the nineteenth-century nation idea of independent states competing for privilege and ascendancy. But the unifying technology of communications did not advance alone: it was accompanied by the technology of annihilation, and both have outrun the usefulness of competition between states. When competition turns to conflict, the heat becomes too intense. To quote Bertrand Russell: "Science has made unrestricted national sovereignty incompatible with human survival. The only possibilities now are world government or death."

To reflect the reality of today's world, the massive expenditures presently committed to protecting outmoded geographical units must now be transferred to the protection of the world itself through transnational institutions of cooperation and security.

The United Nations of 159 countries is the one institution which represents all of humanity. But it has not the regulatory teeth needed to truly influence change, and as Einstein once observed, it is our *thinking* which is most in need of change. Through the ages we have gradually been thinking ourselves — through tribes, cities, provinces, and nations — into larger and larger units of political security. With each new technology the time it has taken to travel or communicate between separate units has decreased. And with instant global communications now in place, we are finally equipped to take the ultimate unifying step.

Sovereign-nation thinking has by definition divided the world into "us" and "them". It is now fully apparent that it is in our best interests to abandon "us-them" thinking, and to conceive a new world order based on the primacy of the whole — a unified whole which has no outside enemy.

The goal of the World Federalists, who are active in 35 countries, is to elevate the United Nations from a purely recommending agency to a legitimate law-making body with the power to make binding decisions. Nations would then be compelled by world law to settle their differences in a world court, and there would at last exist the institutional means to outlaw war for all time.

With the United Nations highly respected and already in place we have the potential to implement the politics of unity. To meet this potential we need the mass will and the organizational intelligence to conceive the legal framework that will make world unity *work*. Men of courage, good faith, and intelligence must come forth from the worldwide legal profession to take up this challenge and give the world its constitutional tools for survival. But the world in turn must declare its political will to receive them, and that means *all* of us.

Another brilliant though less ambitious initiative for the United Nations was conceived in Canada by Operation Dismantle. This is to run a worldwide referendum of public opinion on nuclear disarmament. The ballot would be worded by the U.N. and conducted by national governments at a convenient time (such as an election) for the country.

When the idea was proposed in 1979 the Canadian prime ministers of the time (and subsequently) declined to carry it before the United Nations General Assembly. It remained for President Louis Alberto Monge of Costa Rica, the world's only totally unarmed country, to officially introduce the concept on the floor of the United Nations.

Gallup Polls have shown that over two-thirds of Americans and 70% of Canadians favor carrying out this referendum in every country in the world. Even the opponents of the concept estimate that if consulted, about 80% of world citizens would wish to see the nuclear nations begin an immediate and balanced process of nuclear disarmament.

This international referendum would give the entire human race a democratic vote on its own survival, but it would also threaten world leaders whose primary concerns are less than democratic. In countries where the national government will not facilitate this vote, state or municipal governments, or even non-governmental organizations, may conduct mini-referenda instead. In the United States there are legal provisions for citizen-initiated referenda at both the municipal and state levels.

There would be no point to this whole exercise unless the Soviets were willing to participate. Fortunately they have gone on record, through an official diplomatic statement made in Canada in 1983, as saying there would be "no reason" not to conduct the referendum in the Soviet Union if it were endorsed by the United Nations.

Getting back to occupational strategies for peace, what about the computer experts? There is a group called Computer Professionals for Social Responsibility which has published a bibliography on computer unreliability and nuclear war.[5] Much networking for peace could be done through a large national organization.

The present stagnation in Western democracy could be on the brink of a miraculous rescue in the form of the home computer. Most homes will soon have one, and they could be readily linked by telephone to a national referendum computer. Every eligible voter could have a registration or "sign-on" number, much like a credit card. People without personal computers could vote from federal electoral offices where the machines would be available.

In a true democracy, government files and reports could be

accessed through a government file database by the same home terminal. Government documents librarians could offer database support through a dial-up system as well. This is not a hopelessly futuristic dream — comparable systems exist already to manage tax, medical, inventory, insurance, security and bibliographic information.

But how unsettling to the powers that be, for a nation to have the unquestionable *means* of accessing files and voting on issues without stepping foot out of doors! It is a matter of replacing the technology of annihilation and terror that has us in chains with a technology of freedom and survival through referendum democracy. But once again, will the political will and the organizational genius emerge in time?

The unprecedented moral outrage of whole nations being threatened by nuclear weapons is felt by elected representatives too, but they are afraid to lead the issue. Some have admitted their inability to act without pressure and have requested the support of their constituents. Voters should therefore be aware of initiatives (either unilateral or bilateral) which may be urged upon their political representatives: 1) a nuclear freeze, which is a halt to all production, testing and deployment of nuclear weapons and their delivery systems; 2) a nuclear moratorium, which is a temporary or limited freeze; 3) a comprehensive test tan against all nuclear blasts; 4) an anti-satellite ban against weapons designed to destroy surveillance and communications satellites; 5) flight-test bans against accurate, destabilizing war-fighting missiles; 6) antisubmarine warfare limits; 7) specific weapons bans or reductions, such as the Cruise; 8) a fissionable material ban; 9) nuclear-free zones, which are geographic areas, both at land and sea, where nuclear weapons are prohibited; 10) on-site inspections of weapons for verification; 11) a no-first-use/no-first-strike declaration by the United States and NATO — Brezhnev made Russia's years ago.

In approaching a politician, it is best to start by writing to ask him what his views are, and what he is doing or not doing about the nuclear weapons situation. If there is no reply, the letter should be followed up publicly, perhaps as an "open letter" to the politician through a local newspaper. If your representative is not responsive to letters, telephone calls, or visits from groups of constituents, then join a political party to make sure that at least one party is involved in the issue of nuclear disarmament. Then, at election time, help set up all-candidates meetings to publicly compare the various positions on disarmament.

Mayors and city councillors may be encouraged (often willingly) to declare their municipalities as nuclear-free zones, and so may state governors and provincial premiers. These symbolic declarations, posted at city limits and state borders, have widespread ongoing impact. They momentarily lighten the heart and loosen some of the repressed fear of holocaust that is blocking action in so many people.

Where jurisdictions have been declared to be nuclear-free, the way opens up for much more campaigning at the local government level. Firetrucks could bear the words "We cannot extinguish nuclear fires", for example, and hospitals might post the reminder, "We have only one bed for every 800 people who would be injured in a nuclear blast." This is basically a matter of public education, and where community concern has already sanctioned a nuclear-free zone, public agencies are in an excellent position to reinforce that awareness.

This kind of campaign can really catch on. Engineers for nuclear disarmament could advertise their businesses with "Engineering skills for construction, not destruction." The sky is the limit when it comes to imagination. Vendors of food products may play on their words: submarine sandwiches could become anti-nuclear submarine sandwiches; a tin of mushrooms might caution "Maybee's marvellous mushrooms (but spare us the cloud!)", and so on.

Anyone who presents a label of any kind can make the point in his or her own way. Labor unions committed to peace may state their position on garment or other labels and signs.

Members of any occupation or organized group may participate in chain letters. One person begins the letter by stating that he/she supports nuclear arms control towards the eventual goal of total bilateral disarmament, and then forwards a copy of the letter to each of ten members of the group, union, or association concerned. Each recipient is asked to write, in turn, to ten other people, and gradually the fan spreads out, raising awareness as it goes.

The awareness and initiative that are needed to end the arms race are qualities of the spirit, and the churches must already know that they have an instrumental role to play in guiding the wisdom of our age.

Human psychic energy is most significantly characterized by the *direction* of its release. It may be released either through love or through the various forms of fear — hatred, anger, and violence. Fear is driving the arms race. In response to this greatest crisis of all time the churches should encourage, as their first and foremost priority, the individual's pursuit of the spirit of love within himself. They should remind people of the great power of prayer, and whether prayer is seen as moving the Creator directly, or as consolidating the Creator's spirit within the individual, it amounts to the same thing — a concentrated focus on the energy of love to meet the challenges of life. And that the arms race is the greatest challenge mankind faces there is no doubt — many people find it too frightening to even discuss, and having erected psychic blocks against it, they bring smaller, more manageable problems to their clergymen. So the churchmen have their work cut out for them, if indeed they have come to terms with their own nuclear fears, and the only way to do *that* is to begin to act.

And finally, it is up to parents everywhere to remember what childhood is, to remember themselves as children, and to see the implicit trust and faith that is born in each child towards its own parents. Then to meet that trust by explaining that yes, we do have a formidable problem to solve, but that man through the ages has been beset by problems — by plagues, wars, and natural disasters, and that he has always come through. This time the problem lies in the evolution of man himself, in his transition from technologically-intelligent creature to self-reflective human being. Our children must see that we are once again working to overcome a threat to our existence, that their own parents are working on it, so that the children of the world and their children after them may live on to share in the birthright of life — the great untold promise of the future.

*　　*　　*

In Appendix VIII there appears a list of human service alternatives to the 800 billion dollars the world is spending annually on military activities. The world's leading player in this theater of madness is the United States of America. With so much of its vast energy proceeding from the cynicism and despair upon which nuclear weapons thrive, a bleakness has entered the American soul. A burden of unease and bewilderment has settled over the country like a dense smog, and has blacked out the light of the American spirit. A Chinese proverb sees it this way:

> "If there is light in the soul,
> There will be beauty in the person.
>
> If there is beauty in the person,
> There will be harmony in the house.
>
> If there is harmony in the house,
> There will be order in the nation.
>
> If there is order in the nation,
> There will be peace in the world."

The key now is to put ourselves in order. The order begins

within the individual, in the moment when he or she stops running, and turns to face the danger. In that moment fear is transformed into hope, whose spirit of courage emboldens others, too. Though it may begin with the smallest of actions, it is a move in the *right direction*, and has all the significance of that instant in time when a critically ill patient stops getting sicker and turns toward recovery. And because the action springs from hope it produces expectation, and with expectation energy builds. Like all energy of any kind it touches people nearby, and ripples outward from person to person as excitement begins to grow.

The world itself is now critically ill, and the medicine it needs is human courage. People must join together everywhere in their own communities to fan the flame of courage that has been all but extinguished by the winds of annihilation. The situation, though grave, is reversible, and it begs for change.

All local groups — be they church, labor, youth, women's, environmental, entertainment or professional — must meet together, and often, to feel and nurture the survival power in one another. And nationally, all organizations of any kind which have adopted resolutions for peace must meet together in one great assembly under one enormous umbrella of purpose, to raise a unified voice that will shake the earth with its determination. When this happens, and it is building, America will have rekindled her democracy with all the light and purpose of the young America of yore.

Quotations from Military Professionals and Statesmen about War and Nuclear Weapons

"Of all the evils to public liberty, war is perhaps the most to be dreaded, because it comprises and develops every other. War is the parent of armies; from these proceed debts and taxes. And armies, and debts, and taxes, are the known instruments for bringing the many under the dominion of the few. In war, too, the discretionary power of the executive is extended; its influence in dealing out offices, honors, and emoluments is multiplied; and all the means of seducing the minds are added to those of subduing the force of the people! No nation could preserve its freedom in the midst of continual warfare."
James Madison, 4th President of the United States, 1809-1817. As quoted in: Tryon Edwards, ed., The New Dictionary of Thoughts *(Standard Book Co., 1959), 713.*

"There is no sensible military use for any of our nuclear forces: intercontinental, theater, or tactical."
Admiral Noel Gayler, U.S. Navy (Ret.) Former Director of the National Security Agency, Commander of all U.S. Forces in the Pacific, and Deputy Director of the Joint Strategic Target Planning Staff. The Washington Post, *June 23, 1981.*

"It is time to realize that no one has ever succeeded in advancing any persuasive reason to believe that any use of nuclear weapons, even on the smallest scale, could reliably be expected to remain limited."
McGeorge Bundy, George F. Kennan, Roberts S. McNamara, and Gerard Smith, "Nuclear Weapons and the Atlantic Alliance," Foreign Affairs 61 *(Spring 1982).*

"The peoples should know the truth about the consequences, ruinous for mankind, which nuclear war would bring."
Chairman Leonid Brezhnev, 26th Communist Party Congress, Moscow, February 1981.

"A nuclear war cannot be won and must never be fought."
President Ronald Reagan, Camp David address, April 14, 1982.

"Can civil defense save a country against an all-out nuclear attack? . . . It is impossible."
Lt. Gen. Mikhail Milshtein, USSR Army (Ret.) Second Congress of International Physicians for the Prevention of Nuclear War, Cambridge, England, April 3, 1982.

"You simply can't fight with nuclear weapons, and the first lesson that we have learned as we build up these arsenals is that they serve no rational military purpose.
". . . Both sides are planning, arming, and training for a nuclear war. We are on a collision course in the name of deterrence. Each side says we are building these weapons to deter nuclear war, we are preparing for a war to have peace. We are going to end up with the weapons themselves starting a war which no one wants. They are going to be uncontrollable and unmanageable in time of crisis or under events of stress, miscalculation, or accident."
Rear Admiral Eugene J. Carroll, Jr., U.S. Navy (Ret.), and currently Deputy Director of the Center for Defense Information in Washington, D.C. Nuclear War: The Search for Solutions. Proceedings of a Conference held at the University of British Columbia, October 19-21, 1984 (Vancouver, B.C.: Physicians for Social Responsibility, 1985), 46-48.

"When people speak to you about a preventive war, you tell them to go and fight it. After my experience, I have come to hate war. War settles nothing."
Dwight D. Eisenhower, 34th President of the United States, 1953-1961.

Appendix I

"Nuclear weapons serve no military purpose whatsoever. They are totally useless — except only to deter one's opponent from using them."
Robert S. McNamara, U.S. Secretary of Defense, 1961-1968.
"The Military role of Nuclear Weapons: Perceptions and Misperceptions," Foreign Affairs 62 (Fall 1983), 79.

"To my mind, the nuclear bomb is the most useless weapon ever invented. It can be employed to no rational purpose . . . It is not even an effective defence against itself . . . I question whether these devices are really weapons at all . . ."
Dr. George F. Kennan, U.S. Ambassador to the Soviet Union, 1952-1953. Speech of Acceptance of the Albert Einstein Peace Prize, May 19, 1981.

"The human tragedy reaches its climax in the fact that after all the exertions and sacrifices of hundreds of millions of people and the victories of the Righteous Cause, we have still not found Peace or Security, and that we lie in the grip of even worse perils than those we have surmounted."
Sir Winston S. Churchill, Prime Minister of the United Kingdom, 1940-45, and 1951-55. The New Dictionary of Thoughts, 714.

"We appeal, as human beings to human beings: Remember your humanity, and forget the rest."
Albert Einstein, in the final week of his life, in his last signed appeal against the development of nuclear weapons.

Suggested Readings in Exercise, Nutrition, and Stress Management

Allen, Robert F. *Lifegain: The Exciting New Program that Will Change Your Health — and Your Life*. Morristown, N.J.: Human Resources Institute, 1981.

Ardell, Donald. *Fourteen Days to a Wellness Lifestyle: The Easy, Effective, and Fun Way to Optimum Health and Total Wellbeing*. Mill Valley, Ca.: Whatever Publishing, 1982.

Bailey, Covert. *Fit or Fat? A New Way to Health and Fitness Through Nutrition and Aerobic Exercise*. Boston: Houghton Mifflin, 1978.

Benson, Herbert, and William Proctor. *Beyond the Relaxation Response*. New York: Berkley Publications, 1985.

Brody, Jane E. *Jane Brody's Nutrition Book: A Lifetime Guide to Good Eating for Better Health*. New York: W.W. Norton, 1981.

Burkitt, Denis. *Eat Right — To Keep Healthy and Enjoy Life More. How Simple Diet Changes Can Prevent Many Common Diseases*. New York: Arco, 1979.

Cantu, Robert C. *Toward Fitness: Guided Exercise for Those with Health Problems*. New York: Human Sciences Press, 1986.

Caplow-Linder, Erna, et al. *Therapeutic Dance/Movement: Expressive Activities for Older Adults*. New York: Human Sciences Press, 1979.

Cooper, Kenneth G. *The Aerobic Program for Total Well-Being: Exercise, Diet & Emotional Balance*. New York: M. Evans & Company, 1982.

Appendix II

Consumer Guide Editors. *Rating the Diets, Nineteen Eighty-Six.* New York: New American Library, 1986.

Darden, Ellington. *Nautilus Nutrition Book.* Chicago: Contemporary Books, 1981.

Davis, Martha, et al. *The Relaxation and Stress Reduction Workbook, 2nd ed.* Oakland, Ca.: New Harbinger, 1982.

Dosti, Rose, et al. *Light Style: The New American Cuisine. The Low Calorie, Low Salt, Low Fat Way to Good Food and Good Health.* San Francisco: Harper & Row, 1982.

Fremes, Ruth, and Zak Sabry. *Nutriscore: The Rate-Yourself Plan for Better Nutrition.* Toronto: Methuen, 1982.

Garnet, Eva Desca. *Movement is Life: A Holistic Approach to Exercise for Older Adults.* Princeton, N.J.: Princeton Book Company, 1982.

Getchell, Bud. *Being Fit: A Personal Guide, 2nd ed.* Indianapolis: Benchmark Press, 1986.

Haas, Robert. *Eat to Win: The Sports Nutrition Bible.* New York: New American Library, 1985.

Hess, Mary Abbott, and Anne Elise Hunt. *Pickles and Ice Cream: The Complete Guide to Nutrition During Pregnancy.* New York: Dell, 1984.

Hope, Jane, and Elizabeth Bright-See. *Everywoman's Book of Nutrition.* Toronto: McGraw-Hill Ryerson, 1982.

Katch, Frank I., and William D. McArdle. *Nutrition, Weight Control, and Exercise, 2nd ed.* Philadelphia: Lea & Febiger, 1983.

Kuntzleman, Charles T., and the Consumer Guide Editors. *Rating the Exercises: How to Choose the Exercise that Suits You Best.* Harmondsworth: Penguin, 1980.

LeShan, Lawrence. *How to Meditate: A Guide to Self-Discovery.* New York: Bantam, 1986.

Lowen, Alexander, and Leslie Lowen. *The Way to Vibrant Health: A Manual of Bioenergetic Exercises.* New York: Colophon Books, 1977.

Mahan, L. Kathleen, and Jane Mitchell Rees. *Nutrition in Adolescence*. St. Louis: Times Mirror/Mosby, 1984.

Masters, Robert, and Jean Houston. *Listening to the Body: The Psychophysical Way to Health and Awareness*. New York: Dell, 1978.

Natow, Annette B., and Jo-Ann Heslin. *Nutrition for the Prime of Your Life*. New York: McGraw-Hill, 1984.

Pease, Victor P. *Anxiety into Energy*. New York: Zebra, 1983.

Pelletier, Kenneth R. *Healthy People in Unhealthy Places: Stress and Fitness at Work*. New York: Delacorte Press/Seymour Lawrence, 1984.

Pelletier, Kenneth R. *Longevity: Fulfilling Our Biological Potential*. New York: Dell, 1982.

Pritikin, Nathan. *Diet for Runners*. New York: Simon and Schuster, 1985.

Pritikin, Nathan. *The Pritikin Program for Diet and Exercise*. New York: Bantam Books, 1980.

Rama, Swami. *A Practical Guide to Holistic Health, Rev. ed.* Honesdale, Pa.: The Himalayan International Institute, 1980.

Robertson, Laurel, et al. *The New Laurel's Kitchen*. Berkeley, Ca.: Ten Speed Press, 1986.

Selye, Hans. *The Stress of Life*. New York: McGraw-Hill. 1978.

Selye, Hans. *Stress Without Distress*. New York: New American Library, 1975.

Sheehan, George A. *Dr. Sheehan on Fitness*. New York: Simon and Schuster, 1984.

Steffny, Manfred, and Rosemarie Breuer. *Running for Women: A Basic Guide for the New Runner*. New York: Macmillan, 1985.

Stewart, Gordon W. *Every Body's Fitness Book: A Simple, Safe, and Sane Approach to Personal Fitness, 2nd ed.* Ganges, B.C.: 3S Publishers, 1982.

Appendix II

Sullivan, James V. *Fitness for the Handicapped: An Instructional Approach.* New York: C.C. Thomas, 1984.

Williams, Melvin H. *Nutrition for Fitness and Sport.* Dubuque, Iowa: William C. Brown, 1983.

Winick, Myron. *For Mothers and Daughters: A Guide to Good Nutrition for Women.* New York: William Morrow, 1983.

Peace Groups

1. General

American Civil Liberties Union
132 W. 43rd St.
New York, NY, 10036
(212) 944-9800

American Friends Service
 Committee
1501 Cherry St.
Philadelphia, PA 19102
(215) 241-7000

American Veterans Committee
1735 DeSales St. NW, 4th Flr.
Washington, DC 20036
(202) 293-4890

Association for Conflict
 Resolution
Box 432, Newington Station
Hartford, CT 06111

Beyond War
222 High St.
Palo Alto, CA 94301
(415) 328-7756

Campaign Against Nuclear War
122 Maryland Ave. NE
Washington, DC 20036
(202) 543-5556
HOTLINE: 800-528-6050,
 ext. 47

Campaign for UN Reform
418 Seventh St. SE
Washington, DC 20003
(202) 546-3965

Center for Defense Information
600 Maryland Ave. SW,
 Ste. 303W
Washington, DC 20024
(202) 484-9490
HOTLINE: (202)-DEFENSE

Center for Innovative
 Diplomacy
644 Emerson St., Ste. 32
Palo Alto, CA 94301
(415) 328-5137

Children's Campaign for a
 Positive Future
626 Portofino Lane
Foster City, CA 94404

Children's Campaign for Nuclear
 Disarmament
14 Everit St.
New Haven, CT 06511
(203) 562-0359

Consider the Alternatives
1411 Walnut St., Ste. 920
Philadelphia, PA 19102
(215) 848-4100

Appendix III

Council for a Livable World
20 Park Plaza
Boston, MA 02116
(617) 542-2282
HOTLINE: (202) 543-0006

Council on Foreign Relations
58 E. 68th St.
New York, NY 10021
(212) 734-0400

Earthstewards Network
6330 Eagle Harbor Dr. NE
Bainbridge Island, WA 98110
(206) 842-7986

Environmental Policy Institute
218 D St. SE
Washington, DC 20003
(202) 544-2600

Federalist Caucus
P.O. Box 19482
Portland, OR 97219
(503) 292-4586

Friends of the Third World
611 W. Wayne St.
Fort Wayne, IN 46802
(219) 422-6821

Fund for Peace
345 E. 46th St.
New York, NY 10017
(212) 661-5900

Global Educational Associates
552 Park Ave. E.
East Orange, NJ 07017
(201) 675-1409

Grandmothers for Peace
2708 Curtis Way
Sacramento, CA 95818
(916) 451-4969

Greenpeace USA
1611 Connecticut Ave. NW
Washington, DC 20009
(202) 462-1177

Ground Zero
P.O. Box 15559
Washington, DC 20003
(202) 638-7402

Ground Zero Pairing Project
P.O. Box 19049
Portland, OR 07219
(503) 245-3519

Holyearth Foundation
6330 Eagle Harbor Dr. NE
Bainbridge Island, WA 98110
(206) 842-7986

The Hunger Project
1388 Sutter, Ste. 400
San Francisco, CA 94109
(415) 928-8700

Institute for Soviet-American
    Relations
1608 New Hampshire Ave. NW
Washington, DC 20009
(202) 387-3034

Interhelp
P.O. Box 331
Northampton, MA 01061
(413) 586-6311

International Alliance of Atomic
    Veterans
Box 32
Topock, AZ 86436
(602) 768-7515

Kids Meeting Kids (KMK)
Box 8H
380 Riverside Dr.
New York, NY 10025

National Action/Research on the
Military Industrial Complex
(NARMIC)
1501 Cherry St.
Philadelphia, PA 19102
(215) 241-7175

National Coalition on Television
Violence
P.O. Box 2157
Champaign, IL 61820
(217) 384-1920

National Peace Institute
Foundation
110 Maryland Ave. NE, #409
Washington, DC 20002
(202) 546-9500

Nuclear Control Institute
1000 Connecticut Ave. NW
Washington, DC 20036
(202) 822-8444

Nuclear Free America
325 E. 25th St.
Baltimore, MD 21218
(301) 235-3575

Nuclear Free Zone Registry
28222 Stonehouse Rd.
Lake Elsinore, CA 92330
(714) 674-6576

Parenting in a Nuclear Age
c/o Bananas
6501 Telegraph
Oakland, CA 94609
(415) 658-7101

Peace Links/Women Against
Nuclear War
747 8th St. SE
Washington, DC 20003
(202) 544-0805

Peacemakers
315 W. Gorham St.
Madison, WI 53703

Planetary Citizens
P.O. Box 2722
San Anselmo, CA 94960
(415) 485-1545

Progressive Space Forum
1724 Sacramento St., #9
San Francisco, CA 94109
(415) 673-1079

SANE
711 G St. SE
Washington, DC 20003
(202) 546-7100

United Campuses to Prevent
Nuclear War
220 I St. NE, Ste. 130
Washington, DC 20002
(202) 543-1505

War Control Planners
P.O. Box 19127
Washington, DC 20036
(202) 785-0708

War Resisters League
339 Lafayette St.
New York, NY 10012
(212) 228-0450

Women's Action for Nuclear
Disarmament (WAND)
New Town Station, Box 153
Boston, MA 02258
(617) 643-6740

Women's International League
for Peace and Freedom
1213 Race St.
Philadelphia, PA 19107
(215) 563-7110

Appendix III

Women Strike for Peace
145 S. 13th St., Rm. 706
Philadelphia, PA 19107
(215) 923-0861

World Citizens Assembly
312 Sutter St., Ste. 506
San Francisco, CA 94108
(415) 421-0836

World Federalist Assn.
P.O. Box 15250
Washington, DC 20003
(202) 546-3950

World Peace Council
Lonnrotinkatu 25 A
00180 Helsinki, 18
Finland

International Registry of World
    Citizens
66 Blvd. Vincent Auriol
Paris 75013

2. Occupational Groups

American Society of
    International Law
2223 Massachusetts Ave. NW
Washington, DC 20008
(202) 265-4313

Architects/Designers/Planners
    for Social Responsibility
225 Lafayette St.
New York, NY 10012
(212) 431-3756

Athletes United for Peace
965 Irving
Montara, CA 94037
(415) 728-5078

Business Executives for National
    Security (BENS)
21 Dupont Circle, 4th Flr.

Washington, DC 20036
(202) 429-0600

The Communicators
354 Congress St.
Boston, MA 02210
(617) 423-7886

Computer Professionals for
    Social Responsibility
P.O. Box 717
Palo Alto, CA 94301
(415) 322-3778

Educators for Social
    Responsibility
23 Garden St.
Cambridge, MA 02138
(617) 492-1764

Federation of American
    Scientists
307 Massachusetts Ave. NE
Washington, DC 20002
(202) 546-3300

Foundation for the Arts of Peace
1918 Bonita Ave., 3rd Flr.
Berkeley, CA 94704
(415) 486-0264

High Technology Professionals
    for Peace
639 Massachusetts Ave., #316
Cambridge, MA 02139
(617) 497-0605

International Assn. of Educators
    for World Peace
P.O. Box 3282, Mastin Lake
    Station
Huntsville, AL 35810
(205) 539-7205
HOTLINE: 800-824-7059

International Physicians
    for the Prevention of

Nuclear War
225 Longwood Ave.
Boston, MA 02115
(617) 738-9404

Lawyers Alliance for Nuclear
Arms Control
43 Charles St.
Boston, MA 02114
(617) 227-0118

Lawyers Committee on National
Policy
225 Lafayette St., Rm. 513
New York, NY 10012
(212) 384-8044

Military Law Task Force/
National Lawyers Guild
1168 Union St., Ste. 202
San Diego, CA 92101
(619) 233-1701

Nurses Alliance for the
Prevention of Nuclear War
P.O. Box 319
Chestnut Hill, MA 02167
(617) 232-5167

Organizing Media Project
605 14th St. NW
Washington, DC 20005
(202) 393-4300

Parents and Teachers for Social
Responsibility
P.O. Box 517
Moretown, VT 05660
(802) 229-0137

Performing Artists for Nuclear
Disarmament (PAND)
225 Lafayette St.
New York, NY 10012
(212) 431-7921

Physicians for Social

Responsibility (PSR)
1601 Connecticut Ave. NW,
Ste. 800
Washington, DC 20009
(202) 939-5750

Psychologists for Social
Responsibility
1841 Columbia Rd. NW, #209
Washington, DC 20009
(202) 745-7084

Student/Teacher Organization to
Prevent Nuclear War
636 Beacon St., #203
Boston, MA 02215
(617) 437-0035

Union of Concerned Scientists
26 Church St.
Cambridge, MA 02238
(617) 547-5552

U.S. Committee Against Nuclear
War
1140 19th St. NW, Ste. 900
Washington, DC 20036
(202) 429-9419

World Peace Through Law
Centre
1000 Connecticut Ave. NW,
Ste. 800
Washington, DC 20036
(202) 466-5428

3. Church Groups

Catholic Peace Fellowship
329 Lafayette
New York, NY 10012
(212) 673-8990

Chuches' Center for Theology
and Public Policy
4500 Massachusetts Ave. NW

Appendix III

Washington, DC 20016
(202) 885-9100

Commission of the Churches on
International Affairs
World Council of Churches
777 UN Plaza
New York, NY 10017
(212) 867-5890

Council on Religion and
International Affairs (CRIA)
170 E. 64th St.
New York, NY 10021
(212) 836-4120

Eighth Day Center for Justice
434 S. Wabash Ave.
Chicago, IL 60605
(312) 427-4351

Fellowship in Prayer
134 Franklin Corner Rd.
Lawrenceville, NJ 08648
(609) 896-3636

Fellowship of Reconciliation
P.O. Box 271
Nyack, NY 10960
(914) 358-4601

Friends Committee on National
Legislation (FCNL)
245 2nd St. NE
Washington, DC 20002
(202) 547-6000

Mennonite Central Committee/
U.S. Peace Section
21 S. 12th St.
Akron, PA 17501
(717) 859-1151

National Interreligious Service
Board for Conscientious
Objectors
800 18th St. NW, Ste. 600

Washington, DC 20006
(202) 293-5962

NETWORK, A Catholic Social
Justice Lobby
806 Rhode Island Ave. NE
Washington, DC 20018
(202) 526-4070

Sojourners
P.O. Box 29272
Washington, DC 20017
(202) 636-3637

World Council of Churches
UN Headquarters Liaison Office
777 UN Plaza
New York, NY 10017
(212) 867-5890

4. Coalition Groups

Citizens Against Nuclear War
1201 16th Ave. NW
Washington, DC 20036
(202) 822-7483

Coalition for a New Foreign and
Military Policy
712 G St. SE
Washington, DC 20003
(202) 546-8400

Council for a Nuclear Weapons
Freeze
456 Massachusetts Ave.
Cambridge, MA 02139
(617) 491-7809

Interfaith Center on Corporate
Responsibility
475 Riverside Dr., Rm. 566
New York, NY 10115
(212) 870-2293

Mobilization for Survival
853 Broadway, Rm. 418

New York, NY 10003
(212) 553-0008

Nuclear Weapons Freeze
Campaign
220 I St. NE, Ste. 130
Washington, DC 20002
(202) 544-0880

People's Anti-War Mobilization
19 W 21st St.
New York, NY 10010
(212) 741-0633

Professionals' Coalition for
Nuclear Arms Control
1616 P St. NW, Ste. 320
Washington, DC 20036
(202) 332-4823

World Peacemakers
2025 Massachusetts Ave. NW
Washington, DC 20036
(202) 265-7582

5. **Canada**

Amnesty International
294 Albert St., Ste. 204
Ottawa, Canada K1P 6E6
(613) 563-1891

Canadian Centre for Arms
Control and Disarmament
151 Slater St., Ste. 710
Ottawa, Canada K1P 5H3
(613) 230-7755

Canadian Peace Alliance
555 Bloor St. W., Ste. 5
Toronto, Ont. M5S 1Y6
(416) 588-5555

Canadian Peace Congress
671 Danforth Ave.
Toronto, Ont. M4J 1L3
(416) 469-3422

Canadian Peace Research and
Education Assn.
25 Dundana Ave.
Dundas, Ont. L9H 4E5

Canadian Physicians for the
Prevention of Nuclear War
1335 Carling Ave., Ste. 210
Ottawa, Canada K1Z 8N8
(613) 725-3911

Children's Crusade for Peace
24 Poplar Ave.
St. John's, Nfld. A1B 1C8
(709) 753-3847

Christian Movement for Peace
427 Bloor St., 2nd Flr.
Toronto, Ont. M5S 1X7

Coalition Against the Cruise
P.O. Box 3887, Station "C"
Ottawa, Ont. K1Y 4M5

Greenpeace Foundation
2623 West Fourth Ave.
Vancouver, B.C. V6K 1P8
(604) 736-0321

Operation Dismantle
Box 3887, Station "C"
Ottawa, Canada K1Y 4M5
(613) 722-6001

Project Ploughshares
450 Rideau St.
Ottawa, Canada K1N 5Z4
(613) 230-0860

Science For Peace
University College
University of Toronto
Toronto, Ont. M5S 1A1
(416) 978-6928

Students Against Global
Extermination

Appendix III

P.O. Box 613
Postal Station NDG
Montreal, Quebec
H4A 3R1

Veterans Against Nuclear Arms
1223 Barrington St.
Halifax, N.S. B3J 1Y2
(902) 422-6770

World Conference on Religion
for Peace (Canada)
11 Madison Ave.
Toronto, Ont. M5R 2S2
(416) 924-9351

World Federalists of Canada
46 Elgin St., Ste. 32
Ottawa, Canada K1P 5K6
(613) 232-0647

6. Directories of Peace Groups

i) The annual publication, *American Peace Directory*, is available from: Institute for Defense and Disarmament Studies, 2001 Beacon St., Brookline, MA 02146, Tel. (617) 734-4216.

ii) The *Arms Control Telephone Directory* of peace groups is available from: Nuclear Arms Educational Service, Box 1102, Stanford University, Stanford, CA 94305.

iii) *The Peace Catalog*, 1984, edited by Duane Sweeney, is available from: Press for Peace, Inc., 5621 Seaview Ave. NW., Seattle, WA 98107.

iv) For information on U.S. corporations with military contracts, contact the National Action/Research on the Military Industrial Complex (NARMIC), 1501 Cherry St., Philadelphia, PA 19102, Tel. (215) 241-7175. This group publishes a state-by-state guide to Cruise/Pershing contractors, plus a catalogue of U.S. foreign military sales.

v) For complete up-to-date information on public affairs organizations of all kinds, consult the current edition of the *Encyclopedia of Associations* (Gale Research Company), available widely in public and university libraries. This is the best current source for peace groups: addresses, date founded, membership, publications, affiliations, and objectives.

Soviet Contact Addresses

USSR-USA Society
House of Friendship with
  Peoples of Foreign Countries
14 Kalinin Prospect
Moscow, USSR 103009

International Friendship Club
Moscow City Pioneer and
  School Children Palace
17 Kosygin St.
Moscow, USSR

Committee of Youth
  Organizations
Bolshoi Komsomolski
Pereulok 8
Moscow, USSR

Committee of Youth
  Organizations
Bogdan Khmelulsky 7/8
Moscow, USSR (for pen pals)
Patriarchy

Soviet Women's Committee
6 Nemirovitcha-Danchenko St.
Moscow, USSR 103009

Acadmeny of Medical Sciences
14 Solyanka Street
Moscow, USSR

Academy of Sciences
14 Leninsky Prospect
Moscow, USSR

Soviet Peace Committee
Prospekt Mira 36
Moscow, USSR

Soviet War Veteran's Committee
4 Gogolevski Bulvar
Moscow, USSR

Minister of Education
Ul. Chernyakhovskoya 9
Moscow, USSR

Assotsiatsiya Sodeistviya
Oon V SSR
Kirovst 24
Moscow, USSR 101000
(United Nations Assn.)

Metropolitan Filaret, Chairman,
  Department for Foreign
  Ecclesiastic Relations of the
  Ul. Kropotkinskaya,
Chisty per. 5
Moscow, USSR

Chairman,
State Committee for Television
  and Radio
Ul. Pyatnitskaya 25
Moscow, USSR

Committee of Physical Culture
  and Sports
Ul. Arkhipova 8
Moscow, USSR

Appendix IV

Gosconcert
Neglinnaya 15
Moscow, USSR
(Cultural Exchange)

In addition to the above addresses, the two following US-based peace groups can be helpful in making contact:

i) The US-USSR Bridges for Peace, Box 710, Emerson House, Norwich, VT 05055, Tel. (802) 649-1000. This group publishes the newsletter *Building Bridges*, and sponsors exchange visits between peace groups.

Esperanto

1. Books on Esperanto

Butler, Montagu C. *Esperanto-English Dictionary*. El Cerrito, Ca.: Esperanto League for North America, 1967.

Butler, Montagu C. *Step by Step in Esperanto*. El Cerrito, Ca.: Esperanto League for North America, 1979.

Cresswell, John, and John Hartley. *Teach Yourself Esperanto*. New York: McKay Co.

Eicholz, R. and V. Eicholz. *Esperanto in the Modern World*. Bailieboro, Ont.: Esperanto Press, 1982.

Wells, J.C. *Esperanto Dictionary*. New York: McKay Co., 1974.

2. Esperanto Associations

Memberships, magazines, and further information are available from the following Esperanto associations:

Esperanto League for North America
Box 1129
El Cerito, CA 94530

Esperanto Language Peace Movement
452 Aldine, #501
Chicago, IL 60507
(312) 549-0982

British Esperanto Association
140 Holland Park Ave.
London, England, W11 4UF

Canadian Esperanto Association
Box 126, St. Beaubien
Montreal, Quebec, H2G 3C8
(514) 495-8442

Universala Esperanto-Asocio
Nieuwe Binnenweg 176
3015 BJ Rotterdam, Netherlands

3. Esperanto tapes
are available from
Esperanto Press,
Bailieboro, Ontario, Canada,
K0L 1B0.

Peace Tax Fund and Conscientious Objectors' Addresses

National Campaign for a World
  Peace Tax Fund
2121 Decatur Place, NW
Washington, DC 20008
(202) 483-3751

Conscience and Military Tax
  Campaign
4354½ University Way, NE,
  Ste. 204
Seattle, WA 98105
(206) 547-0952

Peace Tax Campaign
1A Hollybush Place
London E29QX
England

Conscience Canada
P.O. Box 601, Station E
Victoria, B.C. V8W 2P3
Canada
(604) 384-5532

Peace Tax Campaign
#5 - 56 E. Crescent St.
McMahon's Point, N.S.W.
Australia

Peace Tax Campaign
2 Gloucester St.
Wilton/Wellington 5
New Zealand

Désarmament Nucleaire
23 Rue Notre Dame de Lorette
75009 Paris, France

Central Committee for
  Conscientious Objectors
  (CCCO)
An Agency for Military and
  Draft Counseling
2208 South St.
Philadelphia, PA 19146
(215) 545-4626

Friends Committee on
  War Tax Concerns
P.O. Box 6441
Washington, DC 20009
(202) 387-7635

National War Tax Resistance
  Coordinating Committee
P.O. Box 85810
Seattle, WA 98145

Quaker Council for European
  Affairs
50 Sq. Ambiorix, B-1040
Brussels, Belgium

Pax Christi USA Center on
  Conscience and War
348 E. 10th St.
Erie, PA 16503
(814) 453-4955

Tax Resisters Penalty Fund
P.O. Box 25
N. Manchester, IN 46962
(219) 982-4277

War Resisters International
55 Dawes St.
London SE17 1E2
England

War Resisters League
339 Lafayette St.
New York, NY 10012
(212) 228-0450

War Tax Resistance National Ad
  Campaign
402 S. Glendale
Ann Arbor, MI 48103
(313) 668-8084

Things You Can Do to Promote Peace

1. Select cards and notepaper that bear a peaceful message.
2. Distribute peaceful literature when you hold a garage sale, bake sale, or rummage sale.
3. Support world relief agencies.
4. Make "Peace" banners and carry them in Peace Walks.
5. Read the available literature on peace and disarmament.
6. Watch for television programs on peace and disarmament.
7. Post information about arms and world development on bulletin boards in churches, malls, and schools.
8. Form a peace study group with your neighbors, fellow workers, union members, church group, or professional associates.
9. Create tapes or video cassette programs and exchange them with other groups.
10. Arrange for films and speakers on militarism and disarmament to be brought into your community association, union, study, professional or church groups.
11. Use the words and music of the Peace Prayer, endorsed by Mother Theresa.
12. Wear a peace button, and when people comment on it, offer factual information (e.g., the money from one modern fighter plane could vaccinate two million children against lethal infectious diseases) to illustrate your concern.
13. Learn about Amnesty International, Greenpeace, the World Federalists, Operation Dismantle, Project Ploughshares, and the United Nations, and the role of each in promoting matters of peace and conscience. Give memberships to these or-

ganizations for Christmas and birthdays.

14. Put a peace bumper sticker on your car; it may stimulate discussion in the parking lot and get other people involved.
15. Write your Alderman and Mayor to ask them to vote for a global referendum in your municipality. Remind them that it would fall to municipalities to provide clean water, public health services, transportation, and garbage disposal after a nuclear attack.
16. In Canada, write to the Prime Minister, the Minister of Defence, or the Minister of External Affairs, saying that you endorse a freeze on the development, production and deployment of nuclear weapons, and that you endorse a nuclear weapons free zone. Object to Cruise Missile testing. Ask for a report on their progress in arms control talks. It is convincing to state your opinions originally in your own words. Address: House of Commons, Ottawa, K1A 0A6. No postage required.
17. Write letters to newspapers, magazines, and radio and TV stations when you object to military ads or to violent shows and attitudes. Complain to stores and manufacturers about toys which promote violence.
18. Distribute petitions endorsing a freeze on nuclear weapons and a nuclear weapons free zone. Send these petitions to all levels of government which are involved.
19. Hold the Global Referendum vote in local organizations and churches. For more information, and to report results, write: Operation Dismantle, Box 3887, Station "C", Ottawa, Canada, K1Y 4M5.
20. Write letters of thanks to media and newspaper people who offer informative shows or articles on peace initiatives.
21. Make sure your local school and public libraries are well supplied with current literature on peace, justice, and militarism.
22. Send out peace literature with your regular mail. Give VISA or the oil company a surprise!

23. Arrange for a personal talk with your clergyman to encourage his or her participation in peace work.

24. Organize special events (speakers, seminars, marches, rallies, church services) around special days in the "Peace" calendar:

    April 15: International Non-Nuclear Day

    Mother's Day: originally created to protest war

    August 6th and 9th: Hiroshima and Nagasaki Days

    October 24: United Nations Day

    November 11: Remembrance Day

25. Arrange for your study group to make a statement in the newspaper, or to other groups, committing yourselves to constructive alternatives to militarism.

26. Write letters to the editor of your newspaper to express your local concerns, and what you are doing about them.

27. Write articles on disarmament and seek to have them printed in local newspapers, union papers, co-op news, church and school papers, etc.

28. Form a core of speakers in your community and make their availability known.

29. Create local branches and chapters of national and international peace and professional groups working towards disarmament.

30. Set up displays at conferences, fairs, church and school functions, malls, and other meeting places.

31. Make a "Peace" float for your local parade. Emphasize money from arms going into hunger relief.

32. Arrange for a personal talk with your Mayor, Alderman, Member of Parliament or Congressman, to get his or her support for peaceful initiatives.

33. Consider nonpayment of the military portion of your taxes, and redirect that money to a peace fund. (See Appendix VI for addresses.)

34. Pass this book on to the next person who says there is no

point in worrying about nuclear war because there is nothing you can do about it anyhow.

35. Keep optimism uppermost. Build peace in the world upon
peace in yourself.

The foregoing list is compressed from a somewhat longer list
prepared by the Canadian peace organization, Project Ploughshares, with headquarters at 450 Rideau St., Ottawa, Canada,
K1N 5Z4.

The Price We are Already Paying for the Arms Race

1. The world's annual military expenditure has now topped 800 billion dollars, which is 2.2 billion dollars a day, or 1.5 million dollars a minute.
2. For the price of one modern army tank, 520 classrooms could be provided for 15,000 children.
3. The cost of one nuclear submarine would pay for the education of 16 million children in developing countries.
4. In 1979, the estimate of the value of major arms export was 5 times higher than in 1969, and 12 times higher than in 1959. Two-thirds of the global arms trade involved the transfer of weapons from the industrialized world to the Third World.
5. In the Third World, two million people die each year from vaccine-preventable polio, measles, tuberculosis, diphtheria, and tetanus. Three million children could be immunized with these vaccines for the price of one modern fighter plane.
6. 800 million people suffer from malaria, and one million children die from it each year in Africa alone. The diversion of half a day's military expenditures would finance the entire malaria-control program of the World Health Organization.
7. The successful 10-year smallpox eradication program of the World Health Organization cost the equivalent of 5 hours of the world's annual military expenditures.
8. Every 12 days the world spends 26 billion dollars on "defense". This amount would bring subsistence levels of food, water, education, health, and housing to every person on earth.

These figures may be verified with a calculator after consulting the SIPRI (Stockholm International Peace Research Institute) Yearbook on nuclear arsenals, and other standard sources of health and educational expenditures to be found in any public library. The question arises, precisely what are the inhabitants of this largely hungry and disease-ridden planet being defended *against?*

Strategies for Noncooperation with Nuclearism

As we noted in Chapter One, the nuclear arms race "system" may not be likely to change unless a new force emerges to disrupt it. One such force would be the collective indignation of a large majority of world citizens who emphatically wished to live. The phrase "massive interventionist democracy" has been coined to describe what is now necessary to tip the political scales against the accumulating weight of nuclearism.

Citizens everywhere, even under repressive regimes, can be politically effective in legal, nonviolent ways, but the *will* must first be present. That will does not take shape, however, until it is possible for people to visualize a successful outcome to their political actions.

Most people living in nuclear democracies sense that the race for military supremacy is so entrenched that it could be stopped by nothing short of violent insurrection, which they do not support as law-abiding citizens. So "What can I do?" holds sway.

This framing of the nuclear action alternatives as a choice between impotence and violence rests upon an unexamined assumption regarding the nature of political power. In point of fact there are two distinct ways of looking at political power, and the quality of a democracy — that is, the responsiveness of government towards the wishes of its people — depends utterly upon the degree of popular understanding of these two ways.

The first interpretation is that the government in power is virtually indestructible; that it is solid, durable, and self-perpetuating; and that ordinary people are subordinate to it and dependent upon its decisions, good will, and support.

The second way of looking at government power is just the opposite: that government power is conditional upon the decisions, good will and support of the ordinary people — a support which is subject to withdrawal and is therefore fragile.

In the first view, that government is an independent, invincible "monolith" (a massive solid rock) run by strong men, it is implied that violence is the only way to defeat such power.

But the second view, that government power *is* the power of the people, suggests that the people may at any time withdraw or reclaim the power that has been theirs from the start. In the words of Errol Harris, people do not realize that "... political power is their own power ... Consequently they become its accomplices at the same time as they become its victims ... If sufficient people understood this and really knew what they were about and how to go about it, they could ensure that government would never be tyrannical."[1]

The first assumption, that power is "up there", projects power into a place that requires violent action for substantial change. The second assumption, that power is "down here", requires only the nonviolent withdrawal of the supports that are sustaining the disputed policies.

The interesting thing about these two assumptions is that either can be fulfilled if enough people believe in them. Thus the nature of political power is determined largely by the sophistication of popular beliefs about it, so that the nature of power in any country is a psychological mirror of its inhabitants.

How sophisticated can a people be in relation to political power? This depends upon the degree to which the common man comprehends the ultimate *source* of power, which in turn depends upon the common level of reflection and analysis.

"Nonviolent action is based on the view that political power can be most efficiently controlled *at its sources* ... Relying on destructive violence to control political power is regarded by theorists of nonviolent action as being just as irrational as attempting to use a lid to control steam from a cauldron, while allowing the fire under it to blaze uncontrolled."[2]

The monolithic theory of power ignores this fundamental question of the source of a ruler's power, which depends intimately upon the obedience, cooperation, and assistance of the population. All rulers require the skills, knowledge, labor, advice, and administrative ability of much of the population they govern. Without this majority consent for the ruler to govern, he is continually threatened with weakness, if not collapse.

Failure to understand this principle puts every totalitarian ruler in "the dead-end street where all dictatorships ultimately arrive: kill everyone who is not with you or get out."[3]

Even in a totalitarian society, as in a master-slave relationship, the wielding of power, because it involves obedience as well as orders, is not a one-way street in which commands are inevitably carried out. It is always a two-sided relationship, and "there are limits within which the ruler must stay if his commands are to be obeyed. *These limits are subject to change throughout the history of a society.*"[4] Today's governments are playing dangerously close to the limits of human tolerance for nuclear roulette, an issue which has not yet been universally protested because the people have a very real problem.

The problem is that government, whether democratic or not, is actually only a ruling minority, but because it is organized in a hierarchy it can act in concert. The citizens, however, no matter how numerous they might be in opposition to government policy, are disorganized, and can be dealt with one by one.

The solution, therefore, lies in building general opposition to nuclearism into a unified corporate strategy to promote peace.

This means that everybody, everywhere, who is opposed to nuclear weapons should regard himself or herself as part of a single political force which is desperately in need of unification and organization.

What is urgently needed is a popular *vision* of a "massive interventionist democracy", through which a nationwide (or world-wide) corporate union of churches, youth groups, women's groups, trade unions, peace activist groups, world federalists, professional groups, and many others, can focus massive political pressure upon governments to find peaceful solutions to international problems. The corporate headquarters of a *unified* national (or international) peace movement could educate its members in the many available techniques of nonviolent action, some of which are included in this appendix.

People will not commit themselves to political goals without some expectation of success. They must see that when they withdraw their obedience, cooperation, and assistance in sufficient numbers for long enough, the government loses control. People in Western countries have the power to bring their governments under nuclear control, but they must first understand the *way*. If they have the *will* to prevent nuclear war, they will learn the way.

The film "Gandhi" won the best picture award for 1983. This is significant. Gandhi was particularly aware of the importance of a change in public will as a forerunner to a change in cooperation and obedience. For change to take place, he said, three things must happen: 1)a psychological change in people away from passive submission towards courage and self-respect; 2)a recognition by the people that their support makes government possible; and 3)the development of mass determination to withdraw cooperation and obedience.

People can put these three things together if they know how, and of course knowing how opens up the possibility of success, a possibility which allows hopelessness to be replaced by the courage and determination that are needed to fuel the process.

*　　　*　　　*

Appendix IX

ECONOMIC BOYCOTTING

Consumers may decline to purchase goods or services if they object to the morality of those goods and services. The nuclear weapons industry is vast and pervasive throughout society, using aeronautics, chemistry, electronics, engineering, mathematics, missile technology, navigation, telecommunications, detection, physics, propulsion, military science, fuels development, armaments, and space technology, to name a few of its supporting disciplines. There are, in the United States alone, 25,000 contractors and 50,000 subcontractors in the defense industry.[5]

Many of the companies which profit from the defense industry are directly vulnerable to economic boycotts from the ordinary consumer. For example, there are electronics manufacturers supplying circuitry for nuclear weapons who also prosper from the domestic sales of games, appliances, and home computers.

Consumer boycotts could be organized by those who have researched the defense contract industry. Lists of contractors could be published, alerting consumers to who is producing which nuclear arms components. Lists of "clean" companies could also be compiled, encouraging consumers to buy "non-nuclear". Clean companies in their turn could cooperate with one another to deny government the goods, services, and technological advice it needs to advance nuclear weapons systems.

Tenants may register opposition to nuclear weapons by declining to rent or withholding rents for brief periods in symbolic economic boycotts against state or corporate landlords who are involved in arms production. This should be done respectfully, with a full explanation, by people in apartments, offices, or industrial sites.

Owners and managers have their own potential for influence. Retailers, for example, may choose not to handle the domestic products of a defense contractor. Landlords may decline to rent to pro-military personnel. Merchants may conduct short "General strikes" to raise public consciousness in communities which are economically dependent upon nuclear weapons activities.

Banks, credit unions, and other financial institutions may cut off credit to individuals and firms involved in the nuclear arms industry.

Middlemen, such as suppliers and handlers, may boycott the movement of goods destined for nuclear military use.

All Western governments borrow heavily from the savings of their citizens. If the people ever organized themselves to withdraw this voluntary support of government banks, stocks, and bonds, they could bankrupt a government in short order. The accompanying message would have to be clear: "We want you to start disarmament *now. Do* it!" The news media could work to inform the Soviet *people* of the determination of the American *people* to reverse this suicidal game.

Finally, both as a symbol of protest and as a means of withholding funds from government, ordinary people everywhere may refuse to pay their taxes. Income, property, and sales taxes — and licences — for dogs, cars, radios, fishing, hunting, businesses, and so on. When large numbers of people resist taxes simultaneously it threatens the treasury and the downfall of the regime. Such measures are, of course, illegal, and are usually reserved to express ultimate conflicts between the citizens of a country and the policies of their leaders.

Some of these illegal measures are likely to be countered by police action. Such action may be met with "total personal non-cooperation", a tactic used by conscientious objectors — the refusal to do *anything* but breathe air, in the face of being jailed, taken to court, required to sign papers, make promises to improve, or work towards the war effort. Refusing to even walk when arrested, or "going limp" when carried, is very difficult to cope with, and when persisted in often succeeds in defeating disciplinary action.

Actions by non-nuclear national governments may be taken to influence the nuclear nations. John Foster Dulles, Secretary of

State under President Eisenhower, wrote in 1932: "If any machinery can be set up to ensure that nations comply with their covenant to renounce war, such machinery must be sought primarily in the economic sphere."[6]

An embargo is an order which a non-nuclear government may impose, prohibiting the movement of a nuclear nation's merchant ships into or out of its ports. Not only could such a coalition halt the lateral spread of nuclear weapons, but it could provide a new basis for trade and economic interdependence that would divert production away from planetary militarization and toward genuine human needs. As Dwight Eisenhower said so well in 1953: "Every gun that is made, every warship that is launched, every rocket that is fired, signifies in the final sense a theft from those who hunger and are not fed, those who are cold and are not clothed."

STRIKES

Strikes are possible wherever people are employed by other people. Though most often associated with labor disputes, strikes may also be staged to demonstrate a collective feeling towards social, political, or moral issues. They may be used dynamically to illustrate the withdrawal of support for nuclearism.

In protest or token strikes, workers stop work for a minute, an hour, a day, or even a week to draw attention to a principle. Such a strike was used in a nuclear weapons context during a 15-minute work stoppage by 9 million Belgians at 11:00 on May 8, 1962. This example showed how labor, which is already organized for its own purposes, is in a unique position to call its vast memberships into protest over the nuclear issue. Consider the impact of a unified action by teamsters, steelworkers, mineworkers, shipbuilders, and autoworkers; by construction, textile, and farmworkers. Add to that the associations of teachers, nurses, engineers, social workers, biologists, accountants, lawyers, and librarians. The required organization is continuously in place: what is lacking is the general awareness of a)the nuclear danger; b)the vulnerability of government; and c)the great power of the people to effect change. The more people wake up to these realities, the closer nuclearism will be to its demise.

Anti-nuclear or peace-seeking strikes are all the more effective for their lack of self-interest, though in ultimate terms every human being on earth should be aware that his or her greatest self-interest lies in the elimination of nuclear weapons. Though rates of pay and working conditions loom large and immediate in personal lives, they are minuscule in comparison with the survival problems of a post-nuclear world.

Slowdowns in work undermine productivity, reduce profits, clog bureaucracies, and are tricky for management to counter. But once again, if sufficient numbers are involved this method can clearly demonstrate the silent power and determination of ordinary human beings.

Working-to-rule strikes are a variation of the slowdown, in which the employees meticulously follow all the rules and regulations of the union, the employer, and the contract to such technical perfection that productivity is brought to a virtual standstill.

Selective strikes are those in which workers decline to do certain jobs. Where, for example, it is known by trade unions that certain products and materials are destined for use in nuclear missiles or guidance systems, the workers may be advised of the immorality of assisting in their assembly and transportation, and in this way nuclear-specific jobs may be abandoned. This would have the secondary effect of pressuring manufacturers to seek other kinds of contracts and to withdraw from the arms supply business. The object is to make nuclear arms so unpopular that they become unprofitable.

General strikes are work stoppages against the major industries at the regional, national, or international level. They are most often motivated by a perception of economic hardship, but have also been used to urge political change. Some have even been revolutionary, seeking to overthrow the government in power.

An economic shutdown occurs when labor is joined by management, shopkeepers, businessmen, restaurateurs, and so on, with the result that all economic life in the community comes to a standstill in protest against a universally unacceptable state of affairs. This does not seem too unreasonable a step to take against the invisible nuclear prison that confines all of humanity — against the poison that silently awaits a sudden crisis or an accidental relay to erupt into lethal planetary convulsions.

POLITICAL NONCOOPERATION

Political noncooperation is the temporary suspension, usually by large numbers of people, of the usual obedience and cooperation towards the political authority whose policies violate public opinion. Political authority is confronted, for example, when pacifists actively incite people, by means of speeches and leaflets, to illegally enter a missile base.

Government and its departments are vulnerable to noncooperation. Citizens may be urged not to vote during elections in which the central issue of our time — poised stockpiles of earth-shattering megatons — is scarcely mentioned. The major Western political parties are economically tethered to these monsters, which prompts a conspiracy of silence against the electorate and indeed against life itself. The foremost issue of every future national and state election should be the permanent war economy, an economy which has been gradually emerging to shore up a stagnating capitalism in a West which has for decades been saturated with material goods and with the accompanying insanity of planned obsolescence. But at election time the public is repeatedly barraged with the same old secondary issues: interest rates, oil prices, the federal deficit, the President's or the Prime Minister's image, and so on. During the British general election of 1959, there emerged a "Voters' Veto" campaign, which refused to support any candidate who did not clearly state the intention to vote against nuclear arms in Parliament.

Let us turn now to the nature and techniques of civil disobedience. Civil disobedience is a rather special concept in that it arises from a moral conflict within the individual between the laws of his land and the laws of his own conscience — and it is from the dictates of human conscience that political laws proceed.

This considered and often reluctant disobedience occurs when a person believes that obedience to a particular law would make him an accomplice to an act which is "illegal" according to his own best judgment and standards of behavior.

Civil disobedience, therefore, involves the deliberate but peaceful refusal to obey laws, regulations, ordinances, decrees, and military or police instructions which are regarded as fundamentally wrong or unjust. The paying of taxes for nuclear weapons is the kind of requirement that brings normally law-abiding citizens into serious moral conflict with the law. Far from being frowned upon as a counter-cultural or anti-establishment trend, civil disobedience should be viewed as an available tool for people who have the courage to risk prosecution and disfavor by challenging society in matters of personal conviction.

Where matters of higher conscience are involved, people from many walks of life may exercise the options available to them. For example, the government's own employees, officers, and agents may obstruct immoral policies, either openly with explanations, or in the quiet blocking and delay of downward orders. This stalling and obstruction may be carried out under the guise of compliance or even enthusiasm. Such tactics were used by German scientists to slow the Nazi government's development of the atomic bomb. Government employees may actually resign, or refuse to take employment in the first place.

Sympathizers may assist civil disobedience protesters by withholding from police the whereabouts of, for example, Quakers who have refused to pay taxes. Judges and juries may dilute the full strength of the law through their interpretation and sentencing. Police and military personnel may become lenient and inefficient in disciplining resisters. There is a large element of personal choice in the degree of severity police officers use in dealing with civil disobedience.

International government action, which was examined earlier, has great power to control warlike behavior. The League of Nations Covenant, for example, imposed upon its members the requirement of total international embargo (diplomatic, economic, social, and political) against any country which resorted to war to resolve a conflict. The non-nuclear countries of the world today could at any time join together to declare just such an embargo against the countries who are holding the world as ransom in a cold nuclear war.

Non-nuclear governments may recall their diplomats from nuclear countries, or ask that nuclear nations withdraw in kind; they may even withhold diplomatic recognition of the governments of nuclear nations. They may halt international conferences, meetings, negotiations, sports events, or world fairs in protest against nuclear policies. Non-nuclear countries could decline to attend the United Nations sessions until the nuclear nations actually began disarming. They could even condemn nuclear weapons worldwide, and adopt resolutions to make attendance in the General Assembly conditional upon their removal.

NONVIOLENT INTERVENTION

Intervention, as its name suggests, is more active and disrupting in its effects than is simple noncooperation. Also it tends to force an issue.

Psychological intervention includes actions which are designed, through the endurance of physical suffering or hardship, to demonstrate how committed one feels towards a moral issue.

These exhibitions of self-imposed suffering — such as exposing oneself to the elements, damaging one's own property, or fasting — are intended to put emotional pressure on other people to re-examine their beliefs about the issue at hand.

The fast of moral pressure was used in disarmament campaigns in England during the early 1960's, and there achieved surprising public sympathy and support.

Fasting is a truly enlightening experience in itself. Once the initial hunger has passed, the body begins to feel light and clean and rather free in a new way. As the body settles peacefully into its fast, one is amazed at its remarkable reserves, and a new confidence in the fundamental ease of life begins to take shape. One feels less dependent on the daily routines, less earthbound, and the spirit dances.

This escape from need and compulsion is a memorable experience, one which affirms the essential strength of the human being in the context of a world full of insecurity, material competition, and the supporting violent weapons.

If thousands of people were to take part in a four or five day fast — preferably out of doors in fine weather, perhaps in a large municipal park where authorities were sympathetic, or on private land — the impact, both on the participants and on the general public, could be very beneficial. If many such fasts were to occur across the land, a leaf might turn over in human consciousness.

The "reverse trial" is an intervention in which the accused party in a court action against civil disobedience or non-payment of taxes turns the tables by revealing the prosecutor as more unjust or immoral than the defendant. This requires skill and forethought, but if successful stimulates dramatic publicity and support.

People may use their bodies to physically interfere with a place they are not supposed to be. They may enter a government office or a launch-site, and hold a "sit-in" to obstruct normal operations. "Stand-ins" may take place at the entrances to office buildings, outside meeting halls, or anywhere else that officials who have refused to meet public concerns may be found. A variation is the "mill-in", in which activists wander around for hours in public office buildings and generally disrupt the work.

Protesters may march to a symbolic site, such as a strategic command center, and demand possession of it in a "nonviolent raid". Nonviolent raids are not intended to actually seize or hold such places, but rather to challenge the policies of the authority concerned. If enough people surround a facility, their physical presence may be as effective as actually taking it over.

Nonviolent air raids have interesting possibilities. Aeroplanes or balloons or helicopters may be used to distribute leaflets, messages, food, gifts, and toys to the population of an unfriendly country. Imagine thousands or millions of colorful helium balloons, carrying messages of friendship and goodwill, being released from West Berlin on a Sunday afternoon when the wind was blowing eastward. Official interference from either side with a gesture of such good faith would be tantamount to warmongering.

Nonviolent invasion occurs when protesters enter a strictly forbidden area, such as was done at the rocket sites near Omaha, Nebraska in 1959, and in the U.S. Pacific nuclear test areas in 1958 and 1962. This method involves civil disobedience and the likelihood of arrest.

Anti-nuclear protesters have often used nonviolent interjection, in which a few people sit or lie in the path of a truck or train carrying weapons, in order to interrupt the delivery. The drivers are forced to choose between halting their work and injuring the demonstrators. Nonviolent obstruction takes this one step further, when hundreds or thousands of people position themselves to physically obstruct work, vehicles, police or troops, who again would have to injure or kill the demonstrators to get through.

Finally, government policies may be protested by the nonviolent occupation of properties for which the demonstrators have not paid their rent or taxes. The original violation becomes compounded by trespassing, thereby exerting pressure on both the tax departments and the courts.

SOCIAL INTERVENTION

Social institutions, occasions, and behavior patterns may be used to substitute respect and admiration for opposing cultures, in place of fear and suspicion. For example, teach-ins could be held to pay tribute to the greatness of the Slavic people — to honor their music, literature, drama, and ballet; to admire their athletes; and to recognize the historical stoicism and courage of a hardy northern people. Home discussion groups and home dinner parties featuring Russian food, drink, music, and costumes would help to bring this remote culture alive.

School teachers could humanize the Soviet peoples, both through coursework and the presentation of Russian music and plays. Every seemingly small event that proceeds from faith and is oriented towards unity weakens the grip of fear, suspicion, and violence in the world.

Social services and facilities (such as government departments, public transportation, and telephones) may be overloaded far beyond their capacity as a method of focusing attention on public concerns.

"Stall-ins" reduce legitimate business to a snail's pace, and anything symbolically nuclear can be stalled. Income tax, for example, may be paid to tax cashiers in coin, each person taking hours to count out his dues, accurately and methodically, to the military coffers.

A "speak-in" is the respectful interruption of a meeting already in progress — in a church, theater, or town hall — to call public attention to a matter of greater urgency. "Guerilla theater" is a politically pointed skit or act presented under the same circumstances.

Appendix IX

Women, from Greek times to the present, have supported one another in the resolve to deny lovemaking to their husbands until the men have agreed to stop a war. There is justice to this, as the use of young lives for cannon-fodder not only makes a mockery of the act that begins life, but negates the whole parental investment in children. And in the nuclear age all life is at stake.

Rival social institutions, such as new schools whose curricula embrace the principles of world unity and peaceful negotiation, may be set up to parallel the state or provincial education system. Parallel media systems, such as the press, radio, and TV, may be introduced to rival the major networks, which usually support the status quo. These rival systems may air unifying educational programs, and may be financed by subscription like PBS.

A word is in order here about television. The success of democracy in the Greek "polis" and in the early American colonies was based largely upon public meetings of the townspeople. Here, popular feeling towards matters of urgency or injustice would build and snowball until a unified action would emerge. People experienced their political problems together, and reinforced one another's concerns and proposals. Today, families across the land view world problems from the isolation of their own living-rooms, which makes it impossible for unified solutions to stir and grow. People *alone* with the news feel small and powerless to effect change in a society where personal power has quietly migrated to government, the transnationals, and the media.

What is needed now is a sturdy, robust spirit of determination at the neighborhood level to get a grip on national affairs. This calls for regular town and community meetings in which people can *feel* one another's strength and support. (Senior citizens who recall the use of town meetings to address social and economic problems during the 1930's may be the best qualified people to lead this movement.) It calls for alternative media, and soon it will call for national referendums through electronic home voting, as was discussed in Chapter 13.

ECONOMIC INTERVENTION

It cannot be repeated too often that the national preoccupation with defense, which translates into the permanent war economy, is the single most disruptive factor in American economic life.

One way that the unemployed may protest this is by the "reverse strike", in which people voluntarily do public works, such as road repair and reforestation, without authorization or payment. By thus matching unemployment to neglected domestic services, attention is dramatically focused upon the crippling effects of the impossible quest for a final military superiority. "Star Wars", for example, could consume every dollar in the country if it were played out to its logical end.

In the "stay-in" (or "sit-down") strike, workers halt production but stay on the job, which keeps them in control of the factory while preventing strikebreakers from entering. This method could be used to press for the conversion of arms factories to peaceful purposes.

Many farmers have been bankrupted by high interest rates and the withdrawal of federal support. In protest against an administration which prefers guns to butter, the farmers could nonviolently seize tracts of government farmland, and by the symbolic act of ploughing it declare ownership over these tracts. In sympathy to the plight of the farmer, local unions might offer support through strikes and slow-downs.

Countries which are economically dependent upon the nuclear powers should never forget that their dependence is weakness — a weakness which divides the world into camps — and that the way out is to work together in the development and trading of their own goods and services. The alternative is further escalation in the superpower-dominated world military economy.

POLITICAL INTERVENTION

The overloading of government departments with questions or information in deliberate over-compliance to an offending policy is called a "comply-in". Where, for example, it is required to report a change of address (tax and licensing offices) the office in question may be bombarded with letters such as "I moved from the fifth to the seventh floor", or "I'm going to Australia", followed a few days later by "I've changed my mind; I'm going to New Zealand instead." This excessive deluge of information is a legal method of applying pressure on bureaucracies, which are obliged to file all correspondence. In nuclear matters the tax offices are the most appropriate and vulnerable agencies.

Another way to clog the system is to actively seek imprisonment through the peaceful breaking of a law or regulation. This is particularly effective, for example, where only a few demonstrators have been arrested in the course of a nonviolent occupation, when in fact all have broken the law. The rest may press to be jailed also, thereby supporting their companions, overloading costly prison facilities, and gaining publicity for the cause.

Morally neutral laws, such as those against noxious weeds, free-running dogs, and camping on public beaches, may be disobeyed when the nature of things makes it difficult to disobey a law which is directly related to the issue concerned. General civil disobedience is a desperate and powerful tool, however, and should be used only as a final resort.

If Western democratic governments cannot be brought to heel on the nuclear issue, then their citizens may wish to replace them. At some point new leaderships may emerge to create parallel governments which challenge the legitimacy and popular support of existing policies.

In the United States, for example, all federal governments since 1945 have succumbed to the "necessity" of the arms race, so that the American people have been virtually disenfranchised over the issue. If government continues to resist an increasing popular will to clean up its military act, then the revolutionary development of a spontaneously emerging parallel leadership could become a reality.

Such a dual sovereignty actually developed in Rhode Island in the 1840's. In contrast to the aliveness demonstrated by these early Americans, we have the staleness and pessimism of today's world, which has repressed its feelings towards nuclear annihilation in exchange for "the good life" — fast but synthetic everything. This deadness to reality reveals, as one academic has put it, that "we live in a post-nuclear world even though the bombs have not gone off . . . the nuclear winter is already here; it is a cold winter of the soul . . ."[7] Regarding society's violence today, he goes on: "When governments take the lead in planning the systematic murder of millions of innocent people, all other destructive behavior may become permissible. The justification for this — the activity of another superpower — seems inadequate, especially as the proliferation of nuclear weapons does little to change what is deplored about the alien power's system or intentions."

Man's unique intelligence has set him apart from the animals, largely through technology. But his animal violence remains, though its expression in open conflict would now be technological genocide. Violent impulses can no longer be resolved by acting them out in the physical world. Instead, the solution to violence has shifted to the inner world of reflection and self-awareness.

And a solution must come. We are standing on the threshold of a new door to our evolution; it is the entrance to self-understanding, and we must pass through it or die. The same intelligence that created the bombs must now transcend the animal-man that holds them. The time has come for people everywhere to renounce violence as a reaction to conflict, and to take up in its place the clear, intelligent use of nonviolent action. And that action must be guided by hope and creativity rather than by despair and destruction, so that there will be ever-present willingness to negotiate in optimism and good faith for a more harmonious world.

234

FOOTNOTES

Chapter 1: The Runaway Arms Race

1. The Harvard Nuclear Study Group, *Living with Nuclear Weapons* (Cambridge: Harvard University Press, 1983), 149.

2. William Morris, ed., *The Heritage Illustrated Dictionary of the English Language* (New York: American Heritage and Houghton Mifflin, 1973), 1306.

3. Robert S. McNamara, "The Military Role of Nuclear Weapons," *Foreign Affairs 62* (Fall 1983): 72.

4. United States. Department of Labor. Bureau of Statistics, *The Structure of the U.S. Economy, 1980-1985* (Washington, D.C.: U.S. Government Printing Office, 1975.)

5. See Appendix I, which lists statements from retired military personnel, who while in office could not have spoken out.

6. Jerome D. Frank, "Prenuclear-age Leaders and the Nuclear Arms Race," *American Journal of Orthopsychiatry 52* (October, 1982): 632-634.

7. J.M. Lodal, "Finishing START," *Foreign Policy,* (No. 48, Fall 1982).

8. J.S. Nye, "Needing a Simpler Freeze Proposal," *Boston Globe,* (November 8, 1982).

9. Henry M. Jackson, "Nuclear War and the Hot Line," *Wall Street Journal,* (September 3, 1982).

Chapter 2: A Break in the Vicious Circle

1. The term "psychic numbing" was coined by Robert Jay Lifton in the book, *Indefensible Weapons*, CBC, Toronto, 1982, 101.

2. Jerome D. Frank, *op cit.*, 631.

Chapter 3: How the Bomb Works

1. Samuel Glasstone and Philip J. Dolan, eds., *The Effects of Nuclear Weapons*, 3rd ed. (Washington, D.C.: U.S. Government Printing Office, 1977), 17.

Chapter 4: A Visit to Armageddon

1. Glasstone, *ibid.*, 7.

2. A "rem" is one biological unit of radiation, a dose approximately equal to one "rad", which represents the absorption of 100 ergs of nuclear (or ionizing) radiation per gram of absorbing material.

3. William J. Broad, "Nuclear Pulse (I): Awakening to the Chaos Factor," *Science 212* (May 22, 1981): 1009-1012.

Chapter 5: A Middle-Sized War

1. John Hersey, *Hiroshima* (New York: Alfred A. Knopf, 1946).

2. Stuart H. Shapiro, "A Cruel Sham. Testimony on Resolution Number 695 before the Philadelphia City Council Concerning Nuclear War, April 21, 1982," *Journal of Public Health Policy 3* (June 1982): 122-129.

3. V.W. Sidel, H.J. Geiger, and B. Lown, "The Physician's Role in the Post-attack Period," *New England Journal of Medicine 266* (1962): 1137-1145.

4. C.M. Haaland, C.V. Chester, and E.P. Wigner, *Survival of the Relocated Population of the U.S. after a Nuclear Attack* (Springfield, Va.: National Technical Information Service,

1976), 20-21. (Defense Civil Preparedness Agency Report No. ORNL-5041).

5. P.F. Kluge, "Survivalism," *Geo* 3 (1981): 139.

6. Haaland, *op cit.*, 35.

7. Robert Jay Lifton and Richard Falk, *Indefensible Weapons: The Political and Psychological Case Against Nuclearism* (Toronto, Canadian Broadcasting Corporation, 1982), 41.

8. Paul R. Ehrlich et al., "Long-term Biological Consequences of Nuclear War," *Science 222* (December 23, 1983): 1293.

9. *Ibid.*

10. United States Congress. Office of Technology Assessment, *The Effects of Nuclear War* (Springfield, Va.: National Technical Information Service, 1979), 6.

11. World Health Organization, *Effects of Nuclear War on Health and Health Services* (Geneva, W.H.O., 1984), 140.

12. E.I. Chazov and M.E. Vartanian, "Effects on Human Behavior," *Ambio I* (No. 2-3, 1982): 159.

13. *Ibid.*

14. Robert Jay Lifton, "Psychological Effects of the Atomic Bombings." In: Eric Chivian et al., eds., *Last Aid: The Medical Dimensions of Nuclear War* (San Francisco, W.H. Freeman, 1982), 66.

Chapter 6: The Civil Defense Fraud

1. T.K. Jones, as quoted in an interview with R. Scheer, *Los Angeles Times*, (January 15, 1982), 22.

2. United States. Defense Civil Preparedness Agency, *Information Bulletin: Materials for Presentation in Nuclear Protection, No. 306* (Washington, D.C.: April 26, 1979).

United States. Defense Civil Preparedness Agency, *Information Bulletin: Research Report on Recovery from Nuclear Attack, No. 307* (Washington, D.C.: May 10, 1979).

3. United States. Congress. Committee on Armed Services, *Hearings on Military Posture and H.R. 2970, Part 6: Military Personnel and Civil Defense*, 97th Congress, 1st Session (Washington, D.C.: U.S. Government Printing Office, 1981), 789-797.

4. Jennifer Leaning, "Civil Defense in the Nuclear Age." In: Christine Cassel et al., eds., *Nuclear Weapons and Nuclear War: A Sourcebook for Health Professionals* (New York: Praeger, 1984), 413-414.

5. Eric Chivian, "Ten Assumptions of Civil Defense Plans for Nuclear War," 31st Pugwash Conference, Banff, Alberta, Canada, August 28-September 2, 1981.

6. City of Cambridge, Massachusetts, *Cambridge and Nuclear Weapons: Is There a Place to Hide?* (Cambridge, Mass.: City of Cambridge, 198?), 1.

7. William H. Kincade, "Repeating History: The Civil Defense Debate Renewed," In: *Nuclear Weapons and Nuclear War*, 397-398. (Reprinted from the original paper in *International Security 332* (July 20, 1978): 99-110.

8. Shapiro, "A Cruel Sham," 122.

9. "Star Wars," *Manchester Guardian Weekly 132* (March 24, 1985): 17.

10. David Lorge Parnas, *Software Aspects of Strategic Defense Systems* (Victoria, B.C.: University of Victoria Department of Computer Science, July 1985). (Report DCS-47-IR)

11. This refers to the fluid and ever-changing characteristics of enemy weapons, and to unknown enemy countermeasures which may be designed to foil the system. Even before such developments occur, Parnas finds difficulties: "The system will be required to identify, track and direct weapons towards targets whose ballistic characteristics cannot be known with certainty before the moment of battle. It must distinguish these targets from decoys whose characteristics are also unknown."

Footnotes

Chapter 7: The Nightmare

1. Leon Wieseltier, *Nuclear War, Nuclear Peace* (New York: Holt, Rinehart and Winston, 1983), 35. According to Wieseltier, many Soviet war-fighting scenarios contain this significant clause.

2. As it would be clearly self-defeating to initiate all-out nuclear war to gain new territory, what seems to be involved here is that the Soviet Union is prepared to fight to the bitter end to protect itself from further aggression.

3. Falk, *Indefensible Weapons*, 179.

4. *Ibid*, 177.

5. Wieseltier, *Nuclear War, Nuclear Peace*, 38.

6. Carl von Clausewitz. *On War*, 1832. As quoted in Harry G. Summers, "What is War?" *Harper's* (May 1984): 77.

Chapter 8: The Game

1. Carl G. Jung, *Collected Works, Vol. 9* (Bollingen Series XX), (Princeton: Princeton University Press, 1969), 70-71.

2. The singular importance of this direct observation of the truth will be discussed in more detail in later chapters.

3. A statement made by George Kennan, former U.S. Ambassador to the USSR, dated May 19, 1981. As quoted in: Eric Chivian and Suzanne Chivian, eds., *Last Aid: The Medical Dimensions of Nuclear War* (San Francisco: W.H. Freeman, 1982), 3.

4. United States. Bureau of Census, *Statistical Abstract of the United States, 1986* (Washington: U.S. Government Printing Office, 1985), 336.

5. A good discussion of this possible conversion is available in the final chapter of: Dan Smith and Ron Smith, *The Economics of Disarmament* (London: Pluto Press, 1983).

6. The following books offer interesting evidence regarding evolutionary leaps in the development of consciousness:

Peter Russell, *The Global Brain: Speculations on the Evolutionary Leap to Planetary Consciousness* (Los Angeles: J.P. Tarcher, 1983).
Rupert Sheldrake, *A New Science of Life* (Los Angeles: J.P. Tarcher, 1983).
Ken Keyes, *The Hundredth Monkey*, 2nd ed., (Coos Bay, Oregon: Vision Books, 1985).

Chapter 9: The Classic Forces for Change

1. William Morris, ed., *The Heritage Illustrated Dictionary*, 89.

2. P.D. Ouspensky, *The Fourth Way* (New York: Vintage Books, 1971), 105-114.

3. Peter Russell, *The Global Brain*, 49-51.

4. For a good discussion of dividing the self from its violence, see J. Krishnamurti, *Freedom from the Known* (New York: Harper & Row, 1969), 49-57.

5. This momentum is demonstrated by the widespread popularity of *The Hundredth Monkey*, *The Global Brain*, and *A New Science of Life*.

6. Dwight D. Eisenhower is often quoted for his 1959 remark, "I think people want peace so much that one of these days government had better get out of their way and let them have it."

Chapter 10: The Quality of Aliveness

1. Mark Juergensmeyer, *Fighting with Gandhi* (New York: Harper & Row, 1984), 58.

Chapter 11: Arms Reduction

1. Center for Defense Information, *Force Level Calculator* (Washington, D.C.: Center for Defense Information, 1983).

2. Robert C. Johansen, *Toward a Dependable Peace: A Proposal for an Appropriate Security System* (New York: World Policy Institute, 1983), 7-8.

Footnotes

3. Gene Sharp, *The Politics of Nonviolent Action* (Boston, Mass.: Porter-Sargent, 1973). I am much indebted to this work, which provides a carefully documented catalogue of the history of nonviolent action worldwide.

Chapter 12: Negotiating for Peace

1. Georgi A. Arbatov and Willem Oltmans, *The Soviet Viewpoint* (New York: Dodd, Mead, 1983), 92.

2. Bernard Lown and Yevgeni Chazov, "Realities and Visions," *New Perspectives: Journal of the World Peace Council 16* (No. 6, 1986): 11.

3. Roger Fisher and William Ury, *Getting to YES: Negotiating Agreement Without Giving In* (New York: Penguin Books, 1983).

4. Fisher and Ury, *ibid.*, 14.

5. Gorbachev, Mikhail, *Political Report of the CPSU Central Committee to the 27th Congress of the Communist Party of the Soviet Union* (Moscow: Novosti Press, 1986).

6. Gorbachev, Mikhail, *The Moratorium: Selected Speeches and Statements by the General Secretary of the CPSU Central Committee on the Problem of Ending Nuclear Tests (January-September 1986)* (Moscow: Novosti Press, 1986).

7. Arbatov and Oltmans, *op cit.*

8. Lawrence Martin, "The Gorbachev Revolution," *Globe and Mail* (Toronto, March 7, 1987), D1. This summary was taken almost verbatim from an article by the *Globe and Mail* correspondent in Moscow.

9. Carl R. Rogers, *A Way of Being* (Boston: Houghton Mifflin, 1980), 151.

10. Rogers, *ibid.*, 150.

Chapter 13: Individual Opportunities

1. Christine Cassel, et al., eds., *Nuclear Weapons and Nuclear*

War: A Sourcebook for Health Professionals (New York: Praeger, 1984).

2. Ruth Adams and Susan Cullen, eds., *The Final Epidemic: Physicians and Scientists on Nuclear War* (Chicago: Educational Foundation for Nuclear Science, 1981).

3. Eric Chivian and Suzanna Chivian, eds., *Last Aid: The Medical Dimensions of Nuclear War* (San Francisco, W.H. Freeman, 1982).

4. Thomas L. Perry and Diane DeMille, eds., *Nuclear War: The Search for Solutions. Proceedings of a Conference Held at the University of British Columbia, October 19-21, 1984.* (Vancouver: Physicians for Social Responsibility, B.C. Chapter, 1985).

5. Computer Professionals for Social Responsibility, *Computer Unreliability and Nuclear War* (Madison, Wisc.: CPSR, 1983).

Appendix IX

1. Errol E. Harris, "Political Power," *Ethics XLVIII* (October 1957): 10.

2. Gene Sharp, *op cit.*, 10.

3. Mario Rosenthal, *Guatemala: The Story of an Emergent Latin-American Democracy* (New York: Twayne Publishers, 1962), 200.

4. Gene Sharp, *op cit.*, 25. (My italics.)

5. Jim Garrison and Pyare Shivpuri, *The Russian Threat: Its Myths and Realities* (London, Eng.: Gateway Books, 1983), 255.

6. John Foster Dulles, "Practicable Sanctions," in Clark Evans, ed., *Boycotts and Peace* (New York and London: Harper & Bros., 1932), 21.

7. John E. Mack, of Harvard University Department of Psychiatry, as quoted in *The Vancouver Sun* (February 21, 1985).

INDEX

Index

Index

249